Dr. Jaerock Lee was at the threshold of death for seven years as he suffered from a variety of illnesses, but received complete healing when he met the living God. Thereafter, Dr. Lee was called as a servant of God and in 1982 he founded Manmin Church in Seoul, Korea. Manmin has since grown to be a congregation of 120,000 members in the last 31 years. Throughout his ministry, Dr. Lee has manifested the power of God in the name of Jesus Christ and glorified God with miraculous signs and wonders. With countless tangible evidence, God has confirmed time and again the messages Dr. Lee proclaimed wherever he has conducted overseas crusades in many countries including Uganda, Japan, Pakistan, Kenya, the Philippines, Honduras, India, Russia, Germany, Peru, DR Congo, New York City of USA, Israel, and Estonia. These crusades were broadcast to the whole world on television and the Internet. In particular, his powerful ministry at "The 2000 Uganda Holy Gospel Crusade" was featured on CNN (Cable News Network), and at "The 2009 Israel United Crusade" held at the ICC (International Convention Center) in Jerusalem of Israel, he proclaimed Jesus Christ is the Messiah, and this crusade was broadcast live to 220 nations. To this day, Dr. Lee has written 85 books filled with the precious word of life and has led as a myriad of souls to the way of salvation. One of his powerful works, *The Message of the Cross* has awakened a number of souls all over the world from their spiritual slumber.

Around the World

Through the panorama of God's power, he has boldly proclaimed to the world the existence of God, the One and Only Savior of all mankind Jesus Christ, and the truthfulness of all that is recorded in the Bible!

"ចូរក្រោកឡើង ហើយភ្លឺស្វាងចុះ"
(អេសាយ ៦០:១)

"For the earth will be filled with the knowledge of the glory of the LORD, as the waters cover the sea." (Habakkuk 2:14)

Overseas crusades
with Dr. Jaerock Lee
have shaken the world
with the power
of the Holy Spirit

1 Kenya Holy Gospel Crusade
2 Manmin Central Church World Mission
3 Pakistan Great United Crusade
4 Uganda Holy Gospel Crusade
5 Philippine Crusade
6 Honduras Crusade
7 Peru Healing Crusade

Around the World

"You will receive power when the Holy Spirit has come upon you; and you shall be My witnesses both in Jerusalem, and in all Judea and Samaria, and even to the remotest part of the earth." (Acts 1:8)

Overseas crusades
with Dr. Jaerock Lee
have shaken the world
with the power
of the Holy Spirit

1 Democratic Republic of Congo
   Miracle Healing Festival
2 Estonian Miracle Healing Crusade
3 Israel United Crusade
4 New York Crusade
5 Germany Healing Festival
6 Russia Miracle Healing Festival
7 India Miracle Healing Prayer Festival

2

MIRACLE HEALING PRAYER FESTIVAL 2002

JESUS CHRIST HEALS   Revival of God's Power and Authority in the

"Once God has spoken; twice I have heard this: that power belongs to God." (Psalm 62:11)

Overseas crusades
with Dr. Jaerock Lee
have shaken the world
with the power
of the Holy Spirit

Through Dr. Jaerock Lee, whom God affirms with His presence and power, the kind of Biblical healing that is simply impossible by the might of man is taking place even today. At each overseas crusade, countless people have received God's healing of such incurable and terminal diseases as AIDS, cancer, and the like on the spot when Dr. Lee prayed not by placing his hand on each of the sick but merely for all from the pulpit.

1 Israel United Crusade
2 India Miracle Healing Prayer Festival
3 Invited by President of DR Congo Joseph Kabila in 2006

Countless people testified to their miraculous healing

Manmin Central Church

Manmin Central Church takes charge of national evangelization and world mission

As of May 2013, Manmin has 43 branch churches and 13 local sanctuaries in major cities throughout South Korea, and approximately 10,000 overseas branch churches in all corners of the globe. Each worship service at Manmin is broadcast live to its branch churches in Korea and many countries via satellites "NSS-6" (New Skies Satellites 6), ThaiCom 5, Galaxy 19, ABS 1, and GCN, and to the rest of the world on the Internet. In addition, Manmin is actively leading other ministry works including publications of books, newspapers, and magazines, and through performing arts. Manmin has also taken the lead in accomplishing world mission as well as preparing for the mission work in North Korea. Manmin Central Church has also been commissioned to construct the Grand Sanctuary, which will serve to immensely reveal the glory of God.

1 Easter Performance
2 Church Anniversary
3 Nissi Orchestra

4 GCN Launching Ceremony
5 WCDN Conference in 2006

"Arise, shine, for your light has come, and the glory of the LORD has risen upon you." (Isaiah 60:1)

The
MESSAGE
of the
CROSS

The
MESSAGE
of the
CROSS

Dr. Jaerock Lee

URIM
BOOKS

The Message of the Cross by Dr. Jaerock Lee
Published by Urim Books (Representative: Kyungtae Noh)
73, Yeouidaebang-ro 22-gil, Dongjak-Gu, Seoul, Korea
www.urimbooks.com

Unless otherwise noted, all Scripture quotations are taken from the Holy Bible, NEW AMERICAN STANDARD BIBLE, ®, Copyright © 1960, 1962, 1963, 1968, 1971, 1972, 1973, 1975, 1977, 1995 by The Lockman Foundation. Used by permission.

Previously published in Korean by Urim Books, Seoul, Korea in 2002.

First Published December 2003
Second Edition September 2004
Third Edition February 2008
Fourth Edition August 2009
Fifth Edition July 2011
Sixth Edition May 2013
Seventh Edition May 2016

Edited by Dr. Geumsun Vin
Designed by Editorial Bureau of Urim Books
Printed by Yewon Printing Company
For more information contact at urimbook@hotmail.com

PREFACE

Wishing you to understand God's heart and His great plan in love and lay a firm foundation for your faith

The Message of the Cross has led countless people to the way of salvation since 1986 and demonstrated innumerable works of the Holy Spirit through many overseas crusades. At last, God the Father blessed me to publish it. I give all thanks and glory to Him!

Many people say they believe in God the Creator and know the love of His Son Jesus Christ, but are not able to preach the gospel with confidence. In fact, only a few Christians understand the heart and providence of God. Furthermore, some Christians are separated from God because they have neither received clear answers to many questions shown in the Bible nor understood the mysterious providence of the love of God.

For example, what would you say if you are asked the following three questions: "Why did God place the tree of the knowledge of good and evil and let the man eat from the tree?" "Why did God make hell even though He sacrificed His Son

Jesus Christ for sinners?" and "Why is Jesus the only Savior?"

I was not able to understand God's deep providence of creation and His secret providence hidden in the cross during the first several years of my Christian life. After I was called as a minister of the gospel, I began to ask to myself, "How can I lead innumerable people to the path to salvation and glorify God?" It dawned on me that I should understand all the words of the Bible including passages difficult to grasp through the interpretation of God and preach them all over the world. I fasted as often as I could and prayed for this. Seven years passed before God began to reveal them.

In 1985, while I was praying fervently, I was filled with the Holy Spirit. He began to interpret the secret providence of God that had been hidden. It was the "message of cross." I preached it during every Sunday morning service for twenty-one weeks. The cassette tapes on "The Message of the Cross" have influenced countless people inland and overseas. Wherever the message of the cross was preached, the Holy Spirit worked like a blazing fire. Many people repented of their sins and were healed of their diseases or illnesses. They threw away doubts about the providence of God and gained true faith and eternal life. Until then, they did not know God and His deep love exactly. They began to understand God's plan, meet Him, and have hope for an eternal life through this message.

If you understand clearly why God placed the tree of the knowledge of good and evil in the Garden of Eden, you can understand His providence for the human cultivation and love

God even more earnestly. Furthermore, by knowing the true purpose of your life, you will be able to struggle against your sins to the point of shedding the blood, try your best to resemble the heart of the Lord Jesus Christ, and be faithful to God to the point of death.

The Message of the Cross will show you God's secret providence hidden in the cross and help you to lay a firm foundation for a true and good Christian life. Therefore, anyone who reads this book will be able to understand God's deep providence and love, have true faith, and establish and lead a Christian life that is pleasing to His eyes.

I give all my thanks to the director and staff of the Editorial Bureau who have made all efforts to publish this work. I give also thanks to the Translation Bureau.

May countless people understand the deep providence of God, meet God of love, and be saved as true children of God— all this I pray in the name of the Lord Jesus Christ!

Jaerock Lee

INTRODUCTION

The Message of the Cross is the wisdom and power of God, and a powerful message every Christian all over the world must embrace!

I give all thanks and glory to God the Father who has led us to publish *The Message of the Cross*. So many members of Manmin around the world have looked forward to its publishing. This book gives the clear answers to many questions that a lot of Christians have wondered: 'What was God the Creator like before the beginning?' 'Why did God create man and let him live on this earth?' 'Why did God place the tree of the knowledge of good and evil in the Garden of Eden?' 'Why did God send His only begotten Son as an atoning sacrifice?' 'Why did God plan the providence of salvation through the rugged wooden cross?' and to many more questions and more.

This book consists of spirit-filled messages preached by Dr. Jaerock Lee and enlightens you to know and understand the deep, wide, and great love of God.

Chapter 1, "God the Creator and the Bible," introduces God

to you and how He works among you. Through this Chapter you will find evidence of the living God and realize the trueness of the Bible in light of the history of mankind.

Chapter 2, "God Creates and Cultivates Man," testifies that God created all things in the universe and formed man in His image. In addition, this Chapter teaches you the true meaning of human life and the purpose of His raising human beings as His true spiritual children.

Chapter 3, "The Tree of the Knowledge of Good and Evil," provides answers to the fundamental question for all Christians: Why did God place the tree of the knowledge of good and evil? This Chapter explains the reason in detail and helps you understand the deep love and mysterious providence of God who cultivates human beings on earth.

Chapter 4, "The Secret Hidden Before Time Began," explains the relation between the law of the redemption of the land and the spiritual law on human salvation (Leviticus 25). It also explains that all men had to go to the way of death because of their sins but God prepared the wonderful way of their salvation since before time began. Finally, it teaches you why God has hidden the way of human salvation until the time of His choosing and how Jesus is qualified for the conditions of the law of the redemption of the land.

Chapter 5, "Why Is Jesus Our Only Savior?" explains how

God's plan for the human salvation that had been hidden since before time began was fulfilled through Jesus, the reason for His crucifixion, the blessings and rights of children of God, the meaning of the name "Jesus Christ," the reason God gave no other name but Jesus Christ under heaven by which men must be saved, and so forth. You will feel the immeasurable love of God if you understand the spiritual implication of the message depicted in this Chapter.

Chapter 6, "The Providence of the Cross," enlightens you with deep meanings of Jesus' sufferings. Why was Jesus born in the pen of animals and laid in a manger if He were truly the Son of God? Why was He poor all His life? Why was He flogged on all over His body, crowned with thorns, and nailed through on His feet and hands? Why did He suffer from the pain to the point of shedding all His blood and water?

This Chapter provides with exact answers to such questions and helps you understand the spiritual implication of His sufferings. All kinds of diseases and sicknesses as well as problems such as poverty, family discord, business difficulty, and so on will be solved through your understanding and faith in the spiritual meanings of Jesus' sufferings. This Chapter helps you to know such deep love of God, do away with every kind of evil, and participate in the divine nature.

Chapter 7, "The Last Seven Words of Jesus on the Cross," explains the spiritual implication of Jesus' last seven words on the cross just before He died. Through the last seven words on the cross, He fulfilled His mission He had received from His Father God. This Chapter emphasizes that you should understand Jesus' great love for mankind, await His Second Coming, and fight the good fight to the end in hope for resurrection.

Chapter 8, "True Faith and Eternal Life," tells you that we become one with our Bridegroom Jesus Christ only with true faith. The Bible warns of some who say they believe in the Savior Jesus Christ but cannot be saved on the Judgment Day. The Bible places weight not only on accepting Jesus Christ but also on eating the flesh of the Son of Man and drinking His blood to reach eternal salvation. You can have true faith that will lead you to the way of salvation when you eat His flesh and drink His blood. This Chapter also teaches you the nature of true faith, how you obtain it, and what you should do to reach the whole salvation.

Chapter 9, "To Be Born of Water and the Spirit," first mentions the dialogue between Jesus and Nicodemus. This exchange concludes *The Message of the Cross*. Your heart must be renewed continually through water and the Holy Spirit until Jesus Christ returns and you must keep your whole spirit, soul, and body blameless at the Second Coming of the Lord Jesus Christ, the time at which the Lord will receive you as His beautiful bride.

Chapter 10, "What Is Heresy?" delves into the nature of heresy and discusses negative and false understanding many

Christians have on it. Today, many people mistake or blame strong works of God as heretical or wrong carelessly because they do not know the biblical definition of heresy. This Chapter warns you that you should neither blame nor condemn works of the Holy Spirit as heretical and explains how you should distinguish the Spirit of truth and the spirit of falsehood, and about some heretical denominations. Finally, this Chapter emphasizes that you should watch and pray continually and dwell in the truth in order not to fall into temptations of the spirit of falsehood.

The apostle Paul said about the message of the cross, the wisdom of God, in 1 Corinthians 1:18, *"For the word of the cross is foolishness to those who are perishing, but to us who are being saved it is the power of God."* Anyone can have true faith, meet the living God and enjoy a Christian life to the fullest when he understands the secret hidden in the cross and realizes the deep providence of God's great love for mankind.

The Message of the Cross is the basic teaching of your life. Therefore, I pray in the name of the Lord that you may lay the foundation for your Christian life and reach the whole salvation and eternal life.

Geumsun Vin,
Director of Editorial Bureau

CONTENTS

Chapter 1

GOD THE CREATOR AND THE BIBLE

- God Is the Creator
- I Am Who I AM
- God Is Omniscient and Omnipotent
- God Is the Author of the Bible
- Every Word of the Bible Is True

In the beginning
God created the heavens
and the earth.

Genesis 1:1

Many people in this world insist that there is no god. There are also other people who worship gods created by man's imagination or make images of God's creatures and worship them as gods. Even though we cannot see Him, God is surely alive, and there is only the one God whom we have to worship. God is the creator of the universe, of all things, and of mankind. He is the ruler and judge of all things.

What kind of being is God? In fact, it is not easy for man to explain about God. Man is a mere creature. God transcends all limitations of man. God is limitless and without boundaries. No matter how much we contemplate with our knowledge, we cannot fully understand and know about God.

Even though we cannot fully know about God, there are basic things that we have to know as God's children. The fundamental points will be elucidated in detail.

God Is the Creator

Today, there are countless books in the world, but no other book but the Bible gives you the detailed and clear answers to the questions about the origin and creation of the universe, and the beginning and the end of the human race.

The Bible gives a clear answer to the question of the origin of the universe and life. Genesis 1:1 says, *"In the beginning God created the heavens and the earth"* and Hebrews 11:3 reads, *"By faith we understand that the worlds were prepared by the word of God, so that what is seen was not made out of things which are visible."*

Not everything visible was made out of something already in existence. It was created from "nothing" at God's command.

Man can make something out of something else already in existence, namely, transforming or combining materials that are already in existence in order to create something but he cannot create something out of nothing.

It is unimaginable that man could create a living organism. Even if he has developed the scientific technology enough to make artificial intelligence (A.I.) computers or clone lambs, he cannot create even an amoeba out of nothing.

Therefore, people just extract living organisms from things that had been given by God, and combine them in various ways. You must know that it is no more than that.

Thus, you should know that only God is able to create something out of nothing. Only God the Creator created the universe at His command and controls the whole universe, world history, life and death, and the blessings and the curses of mankind.

Evidence That Makes You Believe in God the Creator

Everything–a house, a table, or even a nail–is designed by someone. It goes without saying that there must be the designer of this vast universe. There should be an owner who created it and who governs it. This is God the Creator about whom the Bible repeatedly tells you.

When you look around, there is abundant evidence of creation. For an easy example, consider the tremendous number of people on the earth. Regardless of race, age, gender, social status, and so forth, everyone has two eyes, two ears, one nose with two nostrils, and one mouth.

Even though each animal has a slight difference according to its species, it has the same facial structures. For example, an elephant has a long nose (trunk) but it is in the center of its face, and above its mouth. It is not above its eyes, beneath its mouth, or on the top of its head. Each elephant has two nostrils, two eyes, two ears, and one mouth. All the birds in the air, all the fish in the ocean or in the river, have the same structure.

Not only does each animal share the same facial structure, but each mammal's digestive and reproduction systems are identical as well. In the same way, each consumes food with its mouth and whatever enters the mouth goes into the stomach and comes out of the body. All mammals mate with the opposite sex and give birth to their offspring.

When you put these obvious factors together, you cannot possibly say that it is a coincidence or the evidence of evolution dictated by "the survival of the fittest." None of this can ever be explained by the theory of evolution.

Therefore, the fact that both human beings and animals have the same organic structure suffices as an evidence that everything was created and designed by God the Creator. If God were not the only God but were one among many gods, the creatures would have different numbers of organs and different bodily structures and positions.

Besides, when you take a closer look at nature and the universe, you can find even more proofs of creation in them. How marvelous it is to know that all the things in the solar system such as the earth's revolution and rotation are working without the slightest error!

Look at the watch on your wrist. In it are a great number of elaborate parts. It will not function with even the smallest part missing. Thus, this universe was designed to operate under God's providence.

For instance, neither man nor any other form of life can exist without the moon that is revolving around the earth. The moon could not be positioned a little farther or nearer from the earth than its current position. God placed it at the proper distance so that man can live on the earth.

Because of the current position of the moon, the gravitation of its pull makes the tide and ebb of the sea. This tide creates the sea to be shaken and purified. Likewise, all things in the universe were made to move accurately according to the providence of God.

Why Do Not Some Believe in God the Creator?

Some people believe in God the Creator and live according to His Word. Why do people, who can reason and seek to find answers to everything in science, not believe in God the Creator?

If you have learned that God is alive and the Almighty Creator from faithful Christians since childhood, it would not be difficult to believe in God the Creator.

Yet, today, many of you have been influenced by evolutionism since your adolescent years, and there is so much "knowledge" that is not necessarily all true. You also associate with those who do not believe in God or doubt Him.

After having lived in this environment, if you go to church and hear the Word of God, you are often in doubt and conflict and cannot believe in God the Creator because your prior knowledge contradicts what you learn and hear in church.

As long as you do not get rid of the thoughts or knowledge that you learned in the world even if you attend church regularly, you cannot have spiritual faith–God-generated faith–that is far away from any doubt.

You cannot believe in the heavenly kingdom or hell without spiritual faith. You consider the visible world as the only world, and live in your own ways.

How many times do you see some theories, which had been acknowledged and accepted at the time, reversed or replaced by the new theory afterwards? Even if this is not the exact case, it is true that conventional theories and assertions have been continually revised or supplemented by newly found facts later on.

As time passes and science advances, people make better explanations and theories even if they are not perfect. I would not say the researches by many scientists are all wrong.

There are still many things on the earth that cannot be explained with human capacity, so you must acknowledge this fact.

For example, when it comes to the universe, you have never been to the far side of the universe from the earth, nor have you ever gone back to the ancient times. However, people try to explain the universe by setting up various hypotheses and theories.

Before man went to the moon, we supposed, "There might be some living organisms up there or the organisms might be somewhere in this solar system beyond the earth." Yet, after man's journey to the moon, we announced, "There is no living organism on it." Nowadays, scientists say, "There is a probability of living organism on Mars" or "There are some traces of water on the Red Planet."

Even if you have researched for a long time and increased your knowledge, if you do not know the will, the providence and the power of God the Creator, you end up facing the limitation of human capacity.

Therefore, Romans 1:20 reads that *"For since the creation of the world His invisible attributes, His eternal power and divine nature, have been clearly seen, being understood through what has been made, so that they are without excuse."*

Whoever opens his heart and meditates can feel the power of God and His divine nature through the creatures such as the sun, the moon, and the stars–objects through which God permits you to know His existence and to believe in Him.

I Am Who I AM

Hearing about God the Creator, many people may wonder, "How did He exist at first?" "Where did He come from?" or "With what appearance did He exist?"

Man's knowledge and thought cannot pass a certain limit, which dictates that there should be a beginning and an end of all beings. Therefore, we demand clear answers to such questions. However, God exists beyond human understanding, so He is who "Was," "Is," and "Is To Come."

Exodus 3 portrays a scene in which God commanded Moses to lead the Israelites into the land of Canaan. Moses in turn asked God how he should answer the Israelites should they question him about the name of God.

At this moment, God told Moses, *"I AM WHO I AM,"* and commanded him to say to the Israelites, *"I AM has sent me to you"* (Exodus 3:14).

"I AM" is the phrase that God used to refer to Himself personally, and means that no one gave birth to Him, or created Him, but He is the perfect being, the Creator Himself.

God Was Light with Voice in the Beginning

John 1:1 reads, *"In the beginning was the Word, and the Word was with God, and the Word was God."* In this way, God who was the Word in the beginning was a being who had been in existence perfectly alone without having been created. How and where did He exist?

God is Spirit, so He had been in the form of the Word in the fourth dimension, the spiritual realm, not the third dimension that is visible. God did not exist in any form but as a profound and beautiful light with pure and clear voice, and He ruled over the whole universe.

So, 1 John 1:5 says, *"This is the message we have heard from Him and announce to you, that God is Light, and in Him there is no darkness at all."* It has a spiritual meaning and has an expression of the feature of God who was the Light in the beginning.

In the beginning, God existed as light with voice in it. His voice is pure, sweet, and soft, and rings over the whole universe. Those who have ever heard the voice of God personally could understand this.

God Was Alone Before Time Began

God the Creator had existed before time began, planned to raise His true spiritual children and proceeded with it. Therefore, if you fully come to understand God I AM, you should demolish all your own ways of thinking, theories, and stereotypes and should further accept the work of creation provided by God.

Unlike the things created by God, the things made by man have their limits and flaws. As the knowledge and civilization of human beings advance continuously, better products are being made but they still have plenty of shortcomings.

Some make idols out of gold, silver, bronze, and metal and call them gods before which they bow down and pray for blessings. They are just wooden, metallic, or stony images that cannot breathe, speak, or even blink their eyes (Habakkuk 2:18-19).

Although they claim to be wise, people actually cannot discern between truth and falsehood, but rather make some images and call them their gods that they worship (Romans 1:22-25). How foolish and shameful is this?

Hence, if people have worshiped and served futile gods because they were ignorant of God, they should thoroughly repent of it, worship God I AM, and carry out the duties as His children.

God Is Omniscient and Omnipotent

God the Creator who created the whole universe is the perfect being who existed before the beginning of time, and He is omniscient and omnipotent. The Bible records numerous wonders and miracles that cannot be performed by the power and knowledge of mankind.

These powerful works of the omniscient and omnipotent God who is the same yesterday and today took place during New Testament times as well as Old Testament times through many men of God who had His power.

This is because as Jesus said in John 4:48, *"Unless you people see signs and wonders, you simply will not believe"* people do not believe unless they see the works of the Almighty God.

God Shows Wonderful Miracles and Signs

Exodus records in detail that the omniscient and omnipotent God performed wonderful miracles and signs through Moses as He brought the Israelites out of Egypt into the land of Canaan.

For example, when God sent Moses to Pharaoh, the king of Egypt, He brought forth Ten Plagues on him and his nation, made the Israelites walk on the dry land by dividing the Red Sea and swept the terrified Egyptian army into the surging current.

Even after the Exodus, water came out of a rock when Moses hit it with his staff, bitter water changed into sweet water, and manna came down from heaven so that millions of people could live without any concern for food.

Later on in the Old Testament, we find God empowering Elijah to prophesy three and a half year drought, rain down again through his prayer, and raise the dead.

In the New Testament, we see Jesus, the Son of God, raising Lazarus who had been dead for four days, opening the eyes of the blind, and healing many people with various diseases, infirmities, and evil spirits. He walked on the water and calmed the wind and the waves.

God performed extraordinary miracles by the hands of Paul, so that when handkerchiefs or aprons were even carried from his body to the sick, the diseases left them and the evil spirits went out (Acts 19:11-12). Numerous signs followed Peter who was one of the best disciples of Jesus. People brought the sick into the streets and laid them on beds and mats so that at least Peter's shadow might fall on some of them as he passed by (Acts 5:15).

Besides, God performed wonders and displayed signs through Stephen and Philip in the Bible, and He continues to show them through our church even today.

God Is the Author of the Bible

God is Spirit, so He is invisible but has always shown Himself in many ways. God generally reveals Himself through nature and especially the testimonies of people who are healed and receive answers from Him. He also reveals Himself in detail through the Bible.

Hence, through the Bible, you can know the true One God, meet Him and reach salvation and eternal life by realizing the work of God. In addition, you can live a successful life and give glory to God by understanding the heart of God and realizing how to love Him and how to be loved by Him (2 Timothy 3:15-17).

Scripture Is God-breathed

2 Peter 1:21 says that *"For no prophecy was ever made by an act of human will, but men moved by the Holy Spirit spoke from God,"* and 2 Timothy 3:16 reads *"All Scripture is inspired by God."* This means that the Bible from Genesis to Revelation is the Word of God that was written down only by the will of God.

Therefore, there are many phrases such as "God says," "the LORD says," and "the LORD God says." These confirm that the Bible is not the Word of man but of God.

The Bible has sixty-six books consisting of thirty-nine Old Testament books and twenty-seven New Testament books. The number of writers is estimated at 34. The period of writing the Bible extends from B.C. 1500 to A.D. 100 for about 1,600 years. What is marvelous is that even though many different authors wrote it, the Bible in its entirety is completely coherent from the beginning to the end, and each verse coincides with other verses.

So Isaiah 34:16 reads, *"Seek from the book of the LORD, and read: not one of these will be missing; none will lack its mate. For His mouth has commanded, and His Spirit has gathered them."*

Such could take place because the original writer of the Bible is God, for the Holy Spirit ruled over the hearts of the writers and gathered the Words together. What you should remember is that authors of the Bible are just the ghostwriters who wrote for God and the original writer of the Bible is God.

Let us take an example. Suppose there is an aged mother who

lives in a rural area. She sends a letter to her younger son studying in a city. She is illiterate, so she articulates her message to her older son. When the younger son in the city receives the letter, he would think that his mother sent the letter to him, not that his older brother did, even though it was actually written by his brother. It is the very same with the Bible.

God's Love Letter Full of Blessings and Promises

The Bible was written down by the Spirit-filled servants of God in order to reveal God Himself. You must believe the fact that it is the Word of the faithful God who reveals Himself.

The Word of God is spirit and life (John 6:63), so whoever hears and believes it will gain an eternal life with his soul receiving abundant life. Whoever believes and obeys the Word of God will enjoy a prosperous life and will be a perfect man of God taking after Jesus Christ.

God came to the earth in flesh to show Himself to mankind, and that flesh was Jesus. Philip, a disciple of Jesus, was ignorant of this and demanded that Jesus should show him God. He failed to realize that Jesus was God incarnated, as if to fulfill a proverb saying, "The beacon does not shine at its base."

John 14:8 and the following verses introduce the dialogue between Philip and Jesus:

> Philip said to Him, "Lord, show us the Father, and it is enough for us." Jesus said to him, "Have I been so

long with you, and yet you have not come to know Me,
Philip? He who has seen Me has seen the Father; how
can you say, 'Show us the Father'? Do you not believe
that I am in the Father, and the Father is in Me? The
words that I say to you I do not speak on My own
initiative, but the Father abiding in Me does His works"
(John 14:8-10).

Even though Jesus gave convincing evidence that He and
God is one by performing miracles that would have been
impossible without God's power, Philip wanted Jesus to show
him the Father. Jesus told him to believe His teachings with the
evidence of the miracles themselves.

God came to this world in flesh in order to show Himself and
God had the Bible written because it is normally impossible for
people to see Him with human eyes.

Hence, you can have the blessings and answers God promises
in the Bible when you have a precious fellowship with the living
God through the Bible, know His will and providence, and
observe His Word.

Every Word of the Bible Is True

Historical records allow you to have knowledge about the
people or incidents at a specific time in the past. History is an
account of the changes of the times and it makes you know in
detail the specific things, people, or living conditions of those

times.

The history of mankind has proved that the Bible is true. You find yourself seeing that the Bible is historical and realistic, especially when you take a careful look at the incidents, people, places, or customs recorded in the Bible.

Since the Old Testament has indeed been handed down based on objective facts such as important or trivial pieces of information that have occurred to individuals, peoples, or groups from the time of Adam and Eve, Israel has considered the Old Testament as the sacred and historical document of their nation and heritage to this day. Even many historians acknowledge the Bible as a reliable source.

History Proves the Truthfulness of the Bible

First of all, based on the Bible, I would like to share the history of Israel with you and prove that the Word of God in the Bible is true.

Adam the forefather of human beings sinned against God, so his descendants all human beings thereafter have gone to the way of sin and have lived without knowing God, their Creator. Just then, God chose one nation and intended to reveal His will and providence through it.

First, God called Abraham who had the best "field of heart," refined him, and established him as the father of faith. Abraham was the father of Isaac, Isaac the father of Jacob, and God called Jacob "Israel" and made twelve tribes out of his twelve sons.

When Jacob was alive, God moved him to Egypt and enabled

him to make a nation by increasing his descendants and finally led them to the land of Canaan.

God gave Moses the Law during his stay in the wilderness, trained the Israelites to live according to His Word, and led them only by His Word.

After they were led to the land of Canaan, they prospered only when they obeyed the Law. When Israel served idols and committed evil, its national power declined and it suffered from foreign invasions. The Israelites were imprisoned or enslaved. When they repented, their nation was restored. This cycle was repeated over and over again.

Thus, God shows all human beings through the history of Israel that God is alive and He governs everything by His Word.

You can also see that the prophecies in the Bible have been fulfilled and are in the process of being fulfilled. For example, in Luke 19:43-44, Jesus referred to Jerusalem's fall, saying:

> *For the days will come upon you when your enemies will throw up a barricade against you, and surround you and hem you in on every side, and they will level you to the ground and your children within you, and they will not leave in you one stone upon another, because you did not recognize the time of your visitation.*

In these verses, Jesus meant how the city of Jerusalem would be destroyed because of their increasing wickedness. The prophecy was fulfilled in 70 A.D., when General Titus of the Roman Empire made his men build an embankment against

Jerusalem, encircle it, and kill many people inside the wall. This took place just forty years after Jesus' prophecy.

Jesus said in Matthew 24:32, *"Now learn the parable from the fig tree: when its branch has already become tender and puts forth its leaves, you know that summer is near."* The fig tree here symbolizes the nation of Israel, and this parable teaches that Israel will be independent when Jesus' Second Coming is near. At last, history testifies that this Word of God came true when Israel that had fallen in 70 A.D. was miraculously reestablished on May 14, 1948—1900 years after its destruction.

The Prophecy of the Old Testament and Its Fulfillment in the New Testament

I testify that the Word of God in the Bible is true by studying how the prophecy of the Old Testament has been fulfilled during times of the New Testament.

The Law of the Old Testament was not the perfect way of "obtaining God's true children." It was just the shadow of demonstrating God. That is why God had promised the coming of the Messiah throughout the Old Testament. When the time came, He sent Jesus Christ to this world to keep His promise.

It is evident that Jesus came to earth about 2,000 years ago. Western history is largely divided into two groups according to the birth of Jesus. "B.C." stands for *Before Christ,* meaning the history before the time of Jesus, while "A.D." stands for *Anno Domini* that means "in the year of our Lord." Even history itself attests to the birth of Jesus.

Let us first look at Genesis 3:15:

> *And I will put enmity between you and the woman,*
> *and between your seed and her seed; He shall bruise*
> *you on the head, and you shall bruise him on the heel.*

The verse prophesied that our Savior, as the seed of the woman, would come and destroy the authority of death. "Woman" in this passage means Israel. Actually, Jesus came to the earth as a son of Joseph who belonged to the tribe of Judah of Israel (Luke 1:26-32).

Isaiah 7:14 reads, *"Therefore the LORD Himself will give you a sign: behold, a virgin will be with child and bear a son, and she will call His name Immanuel."*

This implies that the Son of God will be sent to atone for the sins of the human race through being conceived by the Holy Spirit. Indeed, Jesus was born of the Virgin Mary by the Holy Spirit (Matthew 1:18-25).

Jesus was prophesied to be born in the region of Bethlehem, as Micah 5:2 reads:

> *But you, Bethlehem Ephrathah, though you are small*
> *among the clans of Judah, out of you will come for me*
> *one who will be ruler over Israel, whose origins are*
> *from of old, from ancient times.*

Fulfilling this Word, Jesus was born in Bethlehem, Judah during the time of King Herod. Even history reaffirms this.

The slaughter of many innocent infants by King Herod at the time of Jesus' birth (Jeremiah 31:15; Matthew 2:16), Jesus' entrance into Jerusalem (Zechariah 9:9; Matthew 21:1-11), and Jesus' ascending into heaven (Psalm 16:10; Acts 1:9) were prophesied and fulfilled accordingly.

In addition, the betrayal of Judas Iscariot, who followed Jesus for three years (Psalm 41:9) and his betraying Jesus for thirty pieces of silver (Zechariah 11:12) were both prophesied and achieved.

You can thus believe that the Bible is true and it is truly the Word of God, especially when you see that all the prophecies in the Old Testament were exactly fulfilled.

Prophecies of the Bible Yet to Be Achieved

God made Jesus Christ our Savior by fulfilling all the prophecies of the Old Testament during times of the New Testament. Every bit of prophecy on Jesus, the course of history for Israel, and the history of mankind were accomplished without a single error. The scrutiny of the world history leads to find that all the words of prophecy in the Bible have come true and will come true.

The prophets both in Old Testament and New Testament times prophesied the rise and fall of a world power, the destruction and rebuilding of Jerusalem, and the future affairs of important persons. Many prophecies in the Bible have been fulfilled and are now being fulfilled, and people are yet to see Jesus' Second Coming, the Rapture, the Millennium Kingdom, and the Judgment of the Great White Throne. Our Lord is now preparing your place as He promised (John 14:2), and He will soon take you to an eternal place.

Our world is now suffering from famines, earthquakes, abnormal weather, and colossal accidents. You should not consider it a coincidence but instead realize that Jesus' Second Coming is drawing near (Matthew 24:3-14). You should reach a whole salvation by being awake and adorning yourself as a bride.

Chapter 2

GOD CREATES AND CULTIVATES MAN

- God Creates Human Beings
- Why God Cultivates Human Beings?
- God Separates the Chaff from the Wheat

"God created man in His own image, in the image of God He created him; male and female He created them. God blessed them; and God said to them, 'Be fruitful and multiply, and fill the earth, and subdue it; and rule over the fish of the sea and over the birds of the sky and over every living thing that moves on the earth.'"

Genesis 1:27-28

At least once in your life, you may ask fundamental questions such as the origin, destination, purpose, and meaning of life. Then you try to obtain answers. Many people try various methods to solve these problems but only pass away without getting any original answers.

World-famous sages such as Confucius, Buddha, or Socrates also strove to obtain these fundamental answers. Confucius focused on morals, which stressed that perfect virtue was regarded as an ethic ideal, and brought up many disciples. Buddha did penance for a long time to be delivered from worldly existence. Socrates pursued the truth in his own way and searched for the true knowledge.

None of them, however, could find a permanent, fundamental solution, reach the genuine truth, or obtain an everlasting life. That was because the truth hidden before the creation of the world is something spiritual that is invisible and intangible. You cannot find clear answers about life until you understand the providence of God the Creator about the human cultivation.

God Creates Human Beings

A mysterious formation of organs and cells and tissues of man's body is immeasurable. God who created man in this manner wants to obtain true children with whom He can share love forever and more. For this purpose, God made man in His image and His likeness and has cultivated man and prepared heaven.

Then, how did God create all things in the universe and form man?

God's Six-day Creation

Genesis 1 well describes the process during which God created the heavens and the earth in six days. God said, *"Let there be light,"* and there was light (v. 3). He then said, *"Let the waters below the heavens be gathered into one place, and let the dry land appear,"* and we know it was so (v. 9). And so forth.

As it is said in Hebrews 11:3, *"By faith we understand that the worlds were prepared by the word of God, so that what is seen was not made out of things which are visible,"* God created the entire universe by His Word.

God created light on the first day, and created the expanse of sky on the second day. On the third day, when God said, *"Let the waters below the heavens be gathered into one place, and let the dry land appear"* (Genesis 1:9), it was so and God called the dry land earth, and the gathering of the waters He called seas.

Then God said, *"Let the earth sprout vegetation: plants yielding seed, and fruit trees on the earth bearing fruit after their kind with seed in them"* (v. 11), the earth brought forth vegetation, plants yielding seed after their kind, and trees bearing fruit with seed in them, after their kind. On the fourth day, He created the sun, the moon, and the stars in the expanse of the sky, and let the sun govern the day and the moon govern the night. On the fifth day, He created the creatures of the sea and every living and moving thing with which the water teems, according to its kinds, and every winged bird according to its kind. On the sixth day, He created livestock, creatures that move along the ground, and wild animals, each according to its kind.

Man Created in the Image of God

God the Creator had prepared an environment for six days in which man could live, and then created man in His image. He blessed the man as the lord of all creatures, and told him to subdue and rule over them.

God created man in His own image, in the image of God He created him; male and female He created them. God blessed them; and God said to them, "Be fruitful and multiply, and fill the earth, and subdue it; and rule over the fish of the sea and over the birds of the sky and over every living thing that moves on the earth" (Genesis 1:27-28).

How, then, did God form man?

Then the LORD God formed man of dust from the ground, and breathed into his nostrils the breath of life; and man became a living being (Genesis 2:7).

In this verse, dust refers to clay. A skillful potter, using clay of quality, makes celadon porcelain or white porcelain of great monetary value. On the contrary, some other potters make unglazed pottery, roofing tiles, or bricks.

The value of a piece of earthenware mainly depends on who made it, how skillfully it was made, what kind of clay was used, and what kind of pottery it is. As the Almighty God the Creator formed man in His image, how beautifully did He do it?

After forming man in His image from the dust, God breathed into his nostrils the breath of life, that is, the living energy. Then man became a living spirit. The breath of life is strength, power, energy, and spirit of God.

God Breathes the Breath of Life into Man

When you think about the process of a fluorescent light's radiating, you can understand more easily the process that a man was created as a living spirit. If you want to make a fluorescent light radiate, you must first prepare a well-fabricated one and then plug it in. However, it cannot radiate until you switch on the electric current.

The television set in your home works the same. You cannot

see anything on the screen before you turn it on, but once on, you can see and hear various kinds of imagery and sounds. You can make images visual on the screen just by switching on the television. However, in the back of the television, elaborate parts are assembled in a very complicated manner.

Likewise, God formed not only man's shape but also the internal organs and bones in him from the dust of the ground. He made veins through which the blood flowed and the nervous system that could fulfill its function perfectly.

God's power can change dust into soft skin if or when He wants. Just as allowing the flow of electricity, He breathed the breath of life into man. Then the blood in him began circulating immediately, and he could breathe and move.

In addition, because God makes memory units in brain cells of men, men input and memorize what they hear and feel in the brain cells. What is input and memorized becomes knowledge, and the knowledge is reproduced as thoughts. When you use the stored knowledge in life, you call it wisdom.

Human beings, though mere creatures, have increased their wisdom and knowledge, and developed an elaborate scientific civilization. Now, they explore the universe and make computers and input massive information in them or replay it and so they benefit tremendously from computers just as God made memory units in brain cells. They have come so far as to make A.I. computers that can recognize letters or man's voice and can communicate with others. They will become more and more developed as time passes.

How much easier it must have been for the Almighty God

the Creator to form man from the dust of the ground and breathe the breath of life to make him a living being! It is so easy for God who can make something out of nothing, but it is so marvelous and unfathomable for man (Psalm 139:13-14).

Why God Cultivates Human Beings?

Jesus teaches us God's providence through many parables. Because the spiritual realm cannot be understood with human knowledge, He used earthly objects in parables to make you understand.

Many of these deal with cultivation. For example, there are the parable of the sower (Matthew 13:3-23; Mark 4:3-20; Luke 8:4-15), the parable of a mustard seed (Matthew 13:31-32; Mark 4:30-32; Luke 13:18-19), the parable of the weeds in the field (Matthew 13:24-30, 36-43), the parable of a vineyard (Matthew 20:1-16), and the parable of the tenants (Matthew 21:33-41; Mark 12:1-9; Luke 20:9-16).

These parables show us that, just as farmers clear land, sow seeds, cultivate them, and harvest produce, God forms and cultivates human beings on the earth and will separate the wheat from the chaff.

God Wants to Share True Love with His Children

God has not only divinity but also humanity. Divinity is the power of omniscient and omnipotent God the Creator Himself, and humanity is the mind of man. Thus, God created and rules over all the universe, human history and lives. He also feels joy, wrath, sorrow and pleasure, and wants to share love with His children.

The Bible shows us so many times that God has the personality like human beings; God rejoices and blesses men when they, created in God's image, do what is right, but He laments and groans in wrath when they commit sins. God's desire to communicate with His children and give them good things is often expressed in the Word of God.

If God had had only the divine characteristics, He need not have rested after the six-day-creation of the universe, and would not have wanted to have a fellowship with us, saying, *"Pray without ceasing"* (1 Thessalonians 5:17), and *"Call to Me and I will answer you, and I will tell you great and mighty things, which you do not know"* (Jeremiah 33:3).

Sometimes you want to be alone, but may be happier at times you are with a likeminded friend who can share his or her love with you. Likewise, God created man in His image because He wants to exchange love with someone. He is cultivating human spirits on this earth because He wants true children who can understand His heart and love Him from their hearts.

God Wants Children Obeying in Their Free Will

Some may wonder why God created human beings and has been raising them even though there are so many obedient angels and the heavenly host in heaven. Yet, most of angels have no human characteristics that are most important in sharing love. In other words, they have no free will to choose by themselves. They obey commands well like robots, but they cannot feel joy, wrath, sorrow, or pleasure as much as human beings. Therefore, they cannot share love with God from the bottom of their hearts.

For example, let us suppose you have two children. One of them only follows your orders without expressing any emotion, opinion, or love like a well-programmed robot. The other sometimes hurts your feelings, but soon regrets his or her acts, clings to you sweetly, and expresses his or her heart in many ways. Then, which one would you love more? Of course, it is the latter.

Let us suppose you have a robot that cooks, cleans the house, and serves you. Even so, you do not love the robot more than your children. No matter how hard the robot may work for you and how helpful it may be, it cannot take the place of your children.

Likewise, God prefers human beings who joyfully obey Him in their free will with reason and emotion rather than angels and the heavenly host, acting like obedient-programmed robots. He gives human beings free will and His Word. Then He teaches them what is good and evil and what the way of salvation or death is. He waits patiently until they become true children.

God's Human Cultivation with Parental Affection

It is written in Genesis 6:5-6 that *"Then the LORD saw that the wickedness of man was great on the earth, and that every intent of the thoughts of his heart was only evil continually. The LORD was sorry that He had made man on the earth, and He was grieved in His heart."*

Does this mean God did not know this fact when He made man? He knew about it, absolutely. God is omniscient and omnipotent so He had known everything before time began. Nevertheless, He created men and has been cultivating them.

If you are parents, you perhaps understand this more easily. How hard it is to give birth to children and raise them! While a woman is pregnant, many kinds of pain such as nausea follow for nine months. At the time of delivery, great pain accompanies the mother. To feed, clothe, and teach children, parents make great efforts and work hard day and night. When children come home late, their parents worry about them. When they get sick, their parents feel much more pain than children do.

Why do parents raise their children despite all such pain and efforts? The reason is parents want objects with which they can share love, namely, who can feel parents' love and love their parents from their hearts. For parents, even such pains provide happiness. Furthermore, if children resemble their parents closely, how lovely they are! Of course, all children cannot be dutiful to their parents. Some children love and respect their parents, but some grieve them.

Likewise, knowing all the pains in raising children, parents do not regard such things as pains. Instead, they make tremendous efforts, expecting their children to grow up well and to be their joy. In the same way, God knew that human beings would disobey, become corrupt, and cause grief, but He also knew that there would be some true children who would share love with Him. Thus, God created human beings and has been raising them willingly.

God Wants to Be Glorified by His True Children

God is cultivating human spirits on the earth not only to obtain true children but also to be glorified through them. God can receive glory from a great company of angels and the heavenly host ever so much. However, what He really wants is to be glorified by His cultivated, true children from the depths of their hearts.

God tells in Isaiah 43:7 that *"Everyone who is called by My name, and whom I have created for My glory, whom I have formed, even whom I have made,"* and instructs you in 1 Corinthians 10:31, *"Whether, then, you eat or drink or whatever you do, do all to the glory of God."*

God is the Creator, Love and Justice. He gave His only begotten Son to save us, and prepared the heavens and eternal life. He is more than worthy to be glorified. Besides, He wants to return the glory to the ones who give glory to Him.

Therefore, you should become true children of God who can share love with Him forever by understanding why God wants to be glorified through His spiritual-cultivated children.

God Separates the Chaff from the Wheat

Farmers cultivate the land because they want to harvest crops in abundance. God also cultivates human spirits on the earth to get true children who not only love and glorify Him from their hearts but also share love with Him in heaven eternally.

There are always both the wheat and the chaff at harvest, so farmers separate the wheat from the chaff, gather the wheat into their barns, and burn up the chaff with fire. In the same way, God will separate the wheat from the chaff at the end of the cultivation of human spirits:

> *His winnowing fork is in His hand, and He will thoroughly clear His threshing floor; and He will gather His wheat into the barn, but He will burn up the chaff with unquenchable fire* (Matthew 3:12).

Therefore, you must believe firmly that God cultivates human spirits on the earth, and in His own time He will gather the wheat—true children—into heaven for eternal life, but burn the chaff with the unquenchable fire of hell.

Then, let us delve further into what sort of men are the wheat and the chaff in God's sight, and what kinds of places heaven and hell are.

The Wheat and the Chaff

The wheat symbolizes those who accept Jesus Christ, walk in

the truth, and share love with God. They are children of the light who recover the lost image of God, and do whatever God commands.

On the contrary, the chaff represents those who do not accept Jesus Christ, or those who claim to believe but do not live by God's Word, following their own evil desires.

1 Timothy 2:4 describes our God as the one *"who desires all men to be saved and to come to the knowledge of the truth."* That is, God wants all men to be the wheat and enter the kingdom of heaven. God is trying to make you realize this in many ways and leading you to the way of salvation. However, some people finally transgress God's will and providence according to their own free will. These people are no better than beasts before God because they have lost man's values.

Farmers burn the chaff in fire or use it as fertilizer because if both the wheat and the chaff gather into the barn, the wheat will become rotten. Therefore, God will not let the chaff in the kingdom of heaven where the wheat will be. Unlike animals, a man has an everlasting spirit because God breathed the breath of life in him when He created him. So God cannot destroy the chaff, or let them amount to nothing.

It is inevitable for God to gather the wheat in heaven and let them enjoy the eternal happiness, and to burn the chaff in the unquenchable fire of hell forever and ever. Thus, you must keep this fact in mind in order not to be thrown into the fire of hell.

The Beauty of Heaven and the Horror of Hell

On the one hand, heaven is too beautiful to be compared to anything in this world. For example, flowers in this world come to wither soon, but flowers in heaven neither wither nor fall off because everything in heaven is everlasting. The roads are made of pure gold that is as clear as glass, the River of Life shining like pure crystal runs through and houses are made of all kinds of brilliant jewels. Everything is speechlessly beautiful (please refer to *Heaven I & II*).

On the other hand, hell is where worms do not die, and the fire is not quenched. Everyone there will be salted with fire (Mark 9:48-49). Moreover, there is the lake of burning sulfur in hell that is seven times as hot as the lake of fire (Revelation 20:10, 15). Unsaved people must live in the lake of unquenchable fire or the lake of burning sulfur forever. How horrible and scary it is to live there eternally (please refer to *Hell*)!

Therefore, Jesus said in Mark 9:43 that *"If your hand causes you to stumble, cut it off; it is better for you to enter life crippled, than, having your two hands, to go into hell, into the unquenchable fire."*

Why must God of love make both the horrible hell and the beautiful heaven? If evil men are allowed to enter a place where those who are good and lovable to God will dwell, it will be painful to the good men and heaven will be polluted by evil. In brief, God made hell because he loves human beings and wants to give His children only the best.

The Judgment of the Great White Throne

Just as a farmer sows seeds and reaps them year after year, God has cultivated human spirits since Adam was driven out of the Garden of Eden and will do so until Jesus comes again.

God showed His will to the forefathers of faith such as Noah, Abraham, Moses, John the Baptist, Peter, and the apostle Paul. Today, He is continuously cultivating human spirits through His ministers and workers. Yet, just as an ending comes necessarily after a beginning, the cultivation of human spirits will not last forever.

2 Peter 3:8 tells us, *"But do not let this one fact escape your notice, beloved, that with the Lord one day is like a thousand years, and a thousand years like one day."* Just as God rested on the seventh day after the six-day-creation of the universe, Jesus' coming and the New Millennium, the period of Sabbath will come after six thousand years since Adam's disobedience. After that, through the Judgment of the Great White Throne, God will allow the wheat to enter heaven and will throw the chaff into the fire of hell.

Therefore, I pray in the name of the Lord Jesus Christ to understand God's providence and love of the cultivation of human beings deeply, lead a blessed life, and glorify God with a fervent hope for heaven.

Chapter 3

THE TREE OF THE KNOWLEDGE OF GOOD AND EVIL

- Adam and Eve in the Garden of Eden
- Adam Disobeyed With His Own Free Will
- The Wages of Sin Is Death
- Why God Placed the Tree of the Knowledge of Good and Evil in the Garden of Eden

Then the LORD God took the man and put him into the garden of Eden to cultivate it and keep it. The LORD God commanded the man, saying, "From any tree of the garden you may eat freely; but from the tree of the knowledge of good and evil you shall not eat, for in the day that you eat from it you will surely die."

Genesis 2:15-17

Those who do not know the Creator God's great love and His deep and profound providence for raising His true children may ask, "Why did God place the tree of the knowledge of good and evil in the Garden of Eden?" "Why did He let the first man go into the way of destruction?" They think man might not have died and would enjoy a happy life forever in the Garden of Eden only if God had not placed the tree there.

Some of them even say things along the lines of "God might not have known in advance that Adam would eat the fruit of the tree of the knowledge of good and evil" because they do not believe God's omniscience and omnipotence. Did He place the tree in the Garden of Eden with poor insight without knowing Adam's future disobedience? Or did God put the tree there on purpose and lead the man to the way of death? Of course not!

Then, why did God place the tree of the knowledge of good and evil in the middle of the Garden of Eden? Why did Adam disobey God's command and fall into the way of death?

Adam and Eve in the Garden of Eden

God formed the man from the dust of the ground and breathed into his nostrils the breath of life, and the man became a living being (Genesis 2:7). A living being is a spiritual being who does not have any kind of knowledge when he is first created. Let us take an easy example. A newborn baby has no wisdom and knowledge. The baby has a memory system in his brain, but has never seen, heard, or been taught anything. So the baby can only act on instinct.

In the same way, Adam had no spiritual wisdom or knowledge when he first became a living being.

Adam Learned the Knowledge of Life from God

God planted a garden in the east, in Eden and put Adam there. God gave Adam knowledge of life and truth one-on-one, walking with him there so that He could have Adam control and manage the Garden of Eden.

Genesis 2:19 reads, *"Out of the ground the LORD God formed every beast of the field and every bird of the sky, and brought them to the man to see what he would call them; and whatever the man called a living creature, that was its name."* Adam was equipped with the knowledge of life enough to rule over all things.

Also, to God it seemed not good for Adam to be alone. Thus, God caused him to fall into a deep sleep to make a suitable helper for him. God took one of the man's ribs and closed up the place with flesh while the man was asleep. Then He created a woman from the rib He had taken out of the man, and brought her to the man. God had the man unite with his wife, and they became one flesh (Genesis 2:20-22).

This was so not because Adam himself felt lonely but because God had been alone for a long period of time before the beginning of time and knew what loneliness was. God's great love and grace led Him to make Adam's helper and He, knowing Adam's situation in advance, blessed the man and his wife to be fruitful, thrive, and fill the earth.

Adam's Long Life in the Garden of Eden

Then, how long did Adam and his wife Eve live in the Garden of Eden? The Bible does not discuss this in detail, but you must know they lived there much longer than most people think.

The Bible tells all these facts in just a few verses. Thus, many people think that Adam ate the forbidden fruit and fell into destruction not long after God put him in the Garden of Eden. Some of them ask, "The Bible says the history of human beings is six thousand years, but how can you explain many fossils dated from several hundred thousand years ago?"

The history of the human cultivation in the Bible is about 6,000 years, beginning from the time when Adam and Eve were driven out of Eden. It does not include the long period during which they had lived in the Garden of Eden. As a long time passed, there had been great geological and geographical changes like crust reaction and several cycles of reproduction and extinction had taken place on this earth.

Just as God blessed Adam and his wife in Genesis 1:28, the first man Adam, before he was cursed, had walked with God and given birth to many children for a long time and filled the Garden of Eden. As the lord of all created things, Adam subdued and managed the earth as well as the Garden of Eden.

Adam Disobeyed With His Own Free Will

God gave Adam and Eve each free will and allowed them to enjoy abundance and joy of the Garden of Eden. Yet, there was one thing that God prohibited. God commanded them not to eat from the tree of the knowledge of good and evil.

If Adam had understood God's deep heart and loved Him truly, he would not have eaten the forbidden fruit because he knew God's command. However, he did not obey this specific command because he did not love God truly.

God placed the tree of the knowledge of good and evil in the Garden of Eden and established the strict law between God and man. He allowed man to keep the command at his own free will. That was because He wanted to gain true children who would obey Him from the depth of their hearts.

Adam Neglected the Word of God

In the Bible, God often promises blessings to those who obey all His commands and heed all His Word (Deuteronomy 15:4-6, 28:1-14). Yet, who obeys all His commands? Even the Bible admits that there are only a few men in the world who can.

God must have taught the first man Adam that he would

enjoy the eternal life and blessings as long as he obeyed God, but would reach the eternal death if he disobeyed God. God warned him not to eat from the tree of the knowledge of good and evil.

Yet, Adam and Eve disregarded the command of God, and ate the forbidden fruit. Satan tried to disturb God's plan of raising true and spiritual children since the beginning. At last, Satan succeeded in tempting them to eat it through the serpent that was craftier than any other wild animals (Genesis 3:1). Adam and Eve disobeyed the command of God. How, then, did Adam disobey the command of God although he was a living spirit and was taught only the truth by God?

In Genesis 2:15, we find that God made Adam manage and take care of the Garden of Eden. Adam received the power and authority from God to govern and guard it. God made him guard it lest the enemy devil and Satan should break in. Nonetheless, Satan did not fail to control the serpent and tempt Adam and Eve through the serpent. How was this possible?

In a word, Satan is an evil spirit that has authority over the kingdom of the air. Satan has no shape. In Ephesians 2:2, Satan is referred to as the prince of the power of the air, of the spirit that is now working in the sons of disobedience.

Because Satan is like radio waves that fly over the air, Satan could control the serpent in the Garden of Eden to tempt Adam and Eve. Genesis 1 shows a repeated special phrase. At the end of each day of creation, the Bible repeats, "God saw that it was good." This phrase was not spoken on the second day when the expanse was made.

Again, Ephesians 2:2 speaks of a time *"in which you*

formerly walked according to the course of this world, according to the prince of the power of the air, of the spirit that is now working in the sons of disobedience." God foreknew that evil spirits would have the authority over the kingdom of the air.

Eve Fell into the Temptation of the Serpent

The serpent is merely one of the animals of the field. How did it succeed in tempting Eve to disobey the command of God?

In the Garden of Eden, men could communicate with all living creatures such as flowers, trees, birds, beasts, and so on. Eve could also communicate with the serpent. Originally, serpents were loved by men and on good terms with them unlike these days. They were so smooth, clean, long, round and wise as to be favored by Eve. They knew her well and pleased her. The case is the same with dogs that are favored by their owners because they are smarter and follow better than any other animals.

Yet, many people say, "Snakes are terrible, poisonous, and disgusting." They dislike snakes almost instinctively because snakes are the ones that deceived the first man Adam and his wife Eve to disobey the command and pushed them into the way of death.

To understand the nature of the serpent, you must know the characteristic of the original ground. Each soil has different ingredients and different compound proportion of them. According to the elements added to the soil, the soil may become good or poor. When God created all kinds of beasts of the field and all sorts of birds of the air, He selected each soil that was proper for each animal (Genesis 2:19).

God did not make the serpent crafty at first. God made it wise enough to be loved by men. Yet, the serpent became crafty after evil nature had come through it. If the serpent had not received Satan's voice but carried out only God's will, it would have become a wise and good animal. Because it listened to and obeyed Satan's voice, however, the serpent became a crafty animal that deceived Eve to fall into death.

Because Eve Changed the Word of God

The serpent knew what God had told Adam: *"From any tree of the garden you may eat freely; but from the tree of the knowledge of good and evil you shall not eat, for in the day that you eat from it you will surely die"* (Genesis 2:16-17). So the serpent asked Eve craftily, *"Indeed, has God said, 'You shall not eat from any tree of the garden'?"* (Genesis 3:1)

How did Eve reply to the serpent?

From the fruit of the trees of the garden we may eat; but from the fruit of the tree which is in the middle of the garden, God has said, "You shall not eat from it or touch it, or you will die" (Genesis 3:2-3).

God gave Adam a clear warning: *"But from the tree of the knowledge of good and evil you shall not eat, for in the day that you eat from it you will surely die"* (Genesis 2:17). He emphasized that they would never be alive if they ate from the tree. However, Eve's response was not as obvious. She only replied vaguely, "You will die." She omitted the word "surely." In other words, she meant, "If you eat the forbidden fruit, you may or may not die."

She did not keep the command of God in her mind and doubted God's Word a little. After the serpent heard her vague and doubtful answer, it rushed into tempting her more tightly. It even distorted the command of God. The serpent said to the woman, "You will not surely die." It began to alter the command of God and encouraged the woman: *"For God knows that in the day you eat from it your eyes will be opened, and you will be like God, knowing good and evil"* (Genesis 3:5). It tempted her again, stimulating her curiosity even further.

Eve Disobeyed in Her Own Free Will

After Satan breathed sinful desires in the woman through her untrue thought, the tree seemed to her different from what she had known until then. Genesis 3:6 reads, *"When the woman saw that the tree was good for food, and that it was a delight to the eyes, and that the tree was desirable to make one wise, she took from its fruit and ate; and she gave also to her husband with her, and he ate."*

She should have driven out the temptation of the serpent flatly and completely. The cravings of sinful man, the lust of her eyes, and the pride of life consumed her, and drove her into the sin of disobedience.

Some say, "Didn't Adam and Eve eat the fruit of the tree of the knowledge of good and evil because they had a 'sinful nature' in them?" They had no sinful nature but only goodness in them before they disobeyed. They had only their own free will by which they could or could not eat the forbidden fruit against the command of God.

As time passed, they neglected the command of God. Then Satan tempted them through the serpent and they surrendered to temptation. In that way, sin came through them and they violated the order God had established.

That is the similar case with children's growth in evil. Even a child who is wicked in deed and word is not always so evil or wicked from his birth. At first, he imitates other children's coarse words or curses without knowing their meaning. Or he may follow a boy striking another, and enjoy striking other boys and seeing them bursting into tears. So he strikes others repeatedly and evil is conceived and grows in him.

In the same way, Adam did not have a sinful nature from the beginning. When he disobeyed the command of God and ate from the tree with his own free will, sin was conceived and evil was established in him.

The Wages of Sin Is Death

Just as God said to Adam, "You must not eat from the tree of the knowledge of good and evil. When you eat of it, you will surely die," Adam and Eve surely died after they ate of the tree. It says in James 1:15, *"Then when lust has conceived, it gives birth to sin; and when sin is accomplished, it brings forth death."*

Romans 6:23 teaches you the law of the spiritual realm about the result of sin, *"The wages of sin is death."* Let us look into how death came to Adam and Eve because of their disobedience.

Death of Their Spirits

God clearly told Adam, "From the tree of the knowledge of good and evil you shall not eat, for in the day that you eat from it you will surely die." Yet, they did not die immediately after they disobeyed the command of God. They lived very long and gave birth to many more children. Then, what was the "death" of which God warned?

He did not mean the death of their bodies but the death of their spirits. Men are created with a spirit that can communicate with God, a soul that is the servant of their spirit, and a body in which their spirit and their soul dwell. 1 Thessalonians 5:23 says that men are composed of a spirit, a soul and a body. When Adam and Eve disobeyed the command of God, their spirits, the master of a man, died.

God is blameless and unblemished, and the Holy One who dwells in an unapproachable light, so sinners cannot be with Him. Adam could communicate with God when he was a living spirit, but could no longer communicate with God after his spirit died because of sin.

The Beginning of Painful Life

The Garden of Eden was a very abundant and beautiful place where there was no worry and anxiety, and Adam and Eve could live there forever eating from the tree of life. But they were driven out of the Garden of Eden after they sinned. From that time on, their troubles and hardships began.

The woman came to have more pain in childbearing. She came to desire for her husband and her husband came to rule over her. Only after the man cultivated the cursed soil with rough, painful toil, could he eat of it all the days of his life (Genesis 3:16-17).

God tells Adam in Genesis 3:18-19, *"Both thorns and thistles it shall grow for you; and you will eat the plants of the field; by the sweat of your face you will eat bread, till you return to the ground, because from it you were taken; for you are dust, and to dust you shall return."* Through these verses, God implies that man must return to a handful of dust.

Because Adam, the forefather of all mankind, committed the sin of disobedience and his spirit died, all his descendants are born as sinners and go to the way of death.

Romans 5:12 records Adam's enduring legacy: *"Therefore, just as through one man sin entered into the world, and death through sin, and so death spread to all men, because all sinned."*

All Men Are Born With the Original Sin

God enables people to be fruitful and increase in number through the seeds of life that He gives them when He makes them. People are conceived by the unification of a sperm and an egg that God gives each man and woman as the seeds of life. Because the sperm or the egg has the characteristics of each parent, the baby conceived by the unification of the sperm and the egg resembles his or her parents' appearances, characters, tastes, habits, favorites, walking postures, and so on.

In that way, Adam's sinful nature has been passed on to all his descendants after Adam the forefather of all men sinned. It is called the "original sin." Adam's descendants are born with the original sin. So all men are inevitably sinners.

Some unbelievers complain, "Why or how on earth am I a sinner? I have committed no sin." Or others ask, "How can Adam's sin be passed on to me?"

Let us take an example of a child. A nursing mother has a child who is not quite a year-old. She breastfeeds another child before her own child's eyes. It is very likely that the baby becomes upset and tries to push away the other baby. If the mother does not stop nursing the other baby or the baby does not stop sucking her breast, her child may shove or strike the mother or the other baby. If the mother continues to give the other baby milk, her own may burst into tears.

Even though no one taught the little baby envy, jealousy, hatred, greed, or striking, the baby has had those evil things in his mind since he was born. This fact explains that men are born with the original sin that is inherited from their parents.

How much more does each person sin on his own throughout lifetime? You must understand that not only sinful actions but also every kind of evil in one's mind is a sin before God who is the light itself. God perceives and watches evil in the mind such as hatred, greed, condemnation, and many more.

Therefore, the Bible tells us that no one will be declared righteous in God's sight by observing the Law and all men fall short of the glory of God because they have sinned (Romans 3:20, 23).

Not Only Man, But Also All Things Cursed

When Adam, who was the lord of all things, sinned and was cursed, the land and all livestock, all beasts of the field and the birds of the air were cursed along with him. Since then, harmful and poisonous insects such as flies or mosquitoes that transmit all kinds of diseases came into being.

The land began to produce thorns and thistles and men could harvest plants for food only through painful toil and by the sweat of their brow. Men were forced to face tears, sorrow, pain, diseases, death and the like because they were cursed on this earth.

Therefore, Romans 8:20-22 reads, *"For the creation was subjected to futility, not willingly, but because of Him who subjected it, in hope that the creation itself also will be set free from its slavery to corruption into the freedom of the glory of the children of God. For we know that the whole creation groans and suffers the pains of childbirth together until now.*"

Then, how was the serpent cursed? In Genesis 3:14, God said to the crafty serpent that tempted men to sin, *"Because you have done this, cursed are you more than all cattle, and more than every beast of the field; on your belly you will go, and dust you will eat all the days of your life."* Serpents, however, do not eat dust but living animals like birds, frogs, mice, or insects. God said clearly, "And dust you will eat all the days of your life." How should you interpret this verse?

The "dust" here symbolizes "men who are made from the dust of the ground" (Genesis 2:7), and "the serpent" stands for the enemy devil and Satan (Revelation 20:2). "Dust you will eat all the days of your life" symbolizes that Satan and the devil devour people who do not live by the Word of God but rather walk in darkness.

Even the children of God face troubles and hardships that Satan and the devil bring if they commit evil and sin against God's will. Today, Satan and the devil prowl around like a roaring lion looking for someone to devour (1 Peter 5:8). If they find one, they will enslave him or her under the curse of sin and drag the person to the way of destruction. If possible, they try to tempt even the children of God.

Satan and the devil tempt those who say, "I believe in God," but are not sure of God's Word, and lead them to the way of death. Usually, Satan and the devil try to tempt you through those closest to you, such as your spouse, friend, and relatives—the way they tempted Eve through the serpent, one of her most beloved pets.

For example, your spouse or friend may ask, "Isn't it enough for you to attend only the Sunday Morning worship service? Do you always have to attend the Sunday evening worship service too?" or "Do you always try your best to gather everyday?" "God perceives and knows even your inner deep heart because He is omniscient and omnipotent. Should you necessarily cry out in prayer?"

God commanded you to remember the Sabbath day and keep it holy (Exodus 20:8), try to gather in the name of the Lord (Hebrews 10:25), and cry out in prayer (Jeremiah 33:3). Satan can neither tempt nor make sin those who dwell in the Word of God completely (Matthew 7:24-25).

Just as it says in Ephesians 6:11, *"Put on the full armor of God, so that you will be able to stand firm against the schemes of the devil,"* you must equip yourself with the Word of truth of God and courageously drive out the enemy devil and Satan by faith.

Why God Placed the Tree of the Knowledge of Good and Evil in the Garden of Eden

God placed the tree of the knowledge of good and evil in the Garden of Eden not to drive men to destruction but to give them true happiness. Not comprehending His deep plan, many people misunderstand the love and the justice of God and even do not believe in God. They live a dull or lifeless life without finding true purpose for their lives.

Why, then, did God place the tree of the knowledge of good and evil in the Garden of Eden and why does that bring you big blessings?

Adam and Eve Did Not Know True Happiness

The Garden of Eden was very beautiful and abundant beyond your imagination. God made all kinds of trees grow out of the ground. They were pleasing to the eye and good for food. In the middle of the Garden were the tree of life and the tree of the knowledge of good and evil (Genesis 2:9).

Why, then, did God place the tree of the knowledge of good and evil in the middle of the Garden along with the tree of life so that it would be seen well? God had never intended to drive them into the way of destruction by tempting them to eat of the tree. There was a providence of God to let us understand relativity through the tree of the knowledge of good and evil and become His true and spiritual children who can feel His heart.

While people experience tears, sorrow, poverty, or diseases, people may think that Adam and Eve must have been very happy in the Garden of Eden because they did not experience pains like tears, sorrow, poverty or diseases in this world. However, people in the Garden of Eden know neither true happiness nor true love because they had not experienced the relativity.

Let us take an example. There are two boys. One was born and grew up in poverty, but the other was born in abundance and enjoyed it. If you give each of them a very expensive toy as a gift, what kinds of response will each of them make? On the one hand, the boy who has grown up in affluence will not be so thankful because he seldom feels the value of the toy. On the other hand, the other boy who has grown up in poverty will be very thankful and regard the toy as very precious.

True Happiness Comes Through Relativity

In the same way, those who experience relative things of freedom or abundance know and enjoy true happiness or true freedom. Unlike the Garden of Eden, there are many relative things in this world. If you wish to know and enjoy the true value of anything, you must experience its relative things. You cannot realize its true value fully until you experience its opposite aspects.

For example, if you wish to know true happiness, you must experience unhappiness. If you wish to know the value of true love, you must experience hatred. You cannot realize the value of your health fully until you are in pain because of diseases or bad health. You will not realize the value of eternal life and will not be thankful to God the Father who prepares for the good heaven until you understand there are surely death and hell.

The first man Adam enjoyed whatever he wished to eat and had the authority to manage all things in the Garden of Eden. He gained all of them without painful toil or the sweat of his brow. For that reason, he did not express gratitude for God who gave all of them nor did he know His grace and love in his heart.

Later, Adam disobeyed the command of God by eating the fruit. He was a living spirit until then, but after he sinned, his spirit died and he became a man of flesh. He and his wife were driven out of the Garden of Eden and came to live on this earth. He began to endure what he had never experienced in the Garden of Eden: tears, sorrow, diseases, pain, misfortune, death, and so on. At last, he came to experience all that are opposite of happiness of the Garden of Eden.

In such a process, Adam and Eve could understand and feel what happiness or unhappiness was like and how valuable the freedom and abundance that God had given them in the Garden of Eden were.

Your life will be meaningless if you live forever without knowing what happiness and unhappiness are. Even if you have hardships now, your life will be more valuable and meaningful if you can feel true happiness later.

For example, even if parents expect that their children will take pain in studying, they still let their children go to school. If they love their children, parents will readily help their children study hard or experience a lot of good things. It is the same case as the heart of God the Father who sent men to this world and cultivates them as His true children through all kinds of experiences.

For that same reason, God placed the tree of the knowledge of good and evil in the Garden of Eden and did not prevent Adam and Eve from eating from it in their own free will. He planned all things so that men would experience all kinds of joy, anger, sorrow and pleasure in this world and become His true children through the human cultivation.

Through painful experiences, they could finally understand

true value and meaning of those things one by one in the depth of their hearts.

Because they will have known and felt true happiness through the human cultivation, God's children will not betray God again unlike Adam did in the Garden of Eden no matter how long the time goes by. Instead, they will love Him more and more greatly, become filled with joy and thanks and give greater glory to Him.

True Happiness in Heaven

God's children who have experienced tears, sorrow, pain, diseases, death and so on in this world will enter the everlasting heaven and enjoy eternal happiness, love, joy and thanksgiving there forever. They will feel the joy of perfect happiness in heaven.

In this fleshly world, everything rots and dies, but there is no rotting, death, tears, and sorrow in the eternal heavenly kingdom. Gold is considered most highly in this world but all roads in New Jerusalem in heaven are made of pure gold. Heavenly houses are made of very beautiful and valuable jewels. How wondrous and beautiful they are!

I had regarded gold or jewels as the most valuable until I met God, but from the time I learned about the eternal heaven, I began to consider everything in this world vain or worthless. Life in this world is a moment compared to the eternal realm. If you truly believe in and hope for the eternal heaven, you will never love this world. Instead, you will only think what you should and could do to save one more person or how you could evangelize all people around the world. You will pile up for yourself rewards in heaven by giving your best offerings to God with all your heart without trying to store up treasures for yourself on earth.

The apostle Paul could make his rough way to the end with joy and thanks, because he saw the third heaven God showed him in a vision. He had to endure tremendous hardships as an apostle for the Gentiles. God showed him the great beauty of heaven and encouraged him to go his way to the last in the hope for heaven. He was beaten with rods, flogged severely, stoned, imprisoned frequently, and shed his blood while preaching the gospel of the Lord. Despite all this, Paul knew all those things would be rewarded greatly beyond description in heaven. In the end, all his hardships were for great heavenly blessings.

Men of God do not hope for this world. They long only for the heavenly kingdom. This world is a moment in the sight of God, but life in the heavenly kingdom is everlasting. There are no tears, or sorrow, or suffering, or death in heaven. So they can always live joyfully hoping for the great prizes God will reward them in heaven according to what they have sown or done.

Therefore, I pray in the name of our Lord Jesus Christ that you will understand the great love and providence of God the Creator and prepare yourself to enter heaven so that you may enjoy an eternal life and true happiness in a stunningly beautiful and glorious heaven.

Chapter 4

THE SECRET HIDDEN BEFORE TIME BEGAN

- Adam's Authority
  Handed Over to the Devil
- The Law of the Redemption of the Land
- The Secret Hidden
  Since Before the Beginning of Time
- Jesus Is Qualified According to the Law

"Yet we do speak wisdom among those who are mature; a wisdom, however, not of this age nor of the rulers of this age, who are passing away; but we speak God's wisdom in a mystery, the hidden wisdom which God predestined before the ages to our glory; the wisdom which none of the rulers of this age has understood; for if they had understood it they would not have crucified the Lord of glory."

1 Corinthians 2:6-8

Adam and Eve were tempted by the serpent in the Garden of Eden, disobeyed the command of God, and ate from the tree of the knowledge of good and evil because they had the desire to be like God in their mind. As a result, they and all their descendants became sinners.

From a human being's perspective, Adam and Eve are thought to have been miserable because they were driven out of the Garden of Eden and would have to go to the way of death. Spiritually speaking, however, it is an amazing blessing of God since they will get the chance to enjoy salvation, eternal life and heavenly blessings through Jesus Christ.

Through the human cultivation, the secret that has been hidden for your glory before the beginning of time was revealed and the way of salvation was opened wide to all nations. Let us delve deeper into the secret that has been hidden before time began and how the way of salvation has been opened.

Adam's Authority Handed Over to the Devil

In Luke 4:5-6, we find the devil tempting Jesus who had just finished a forty-day fasting:

And he led Him up and showed Him all the kingdoms of the world in a moment of time. And the devil said to Him, "I will give You all this domain and its glory; for it has been handed over to me, and I give it to whomever I wish."

The devil said that he would hand over the authority to Jesus because he had been handed over it from someone. Why did God, who governs all things, allow all authority to be handed over to the devil?

It says in Genesis 1:28, *"God blessed them; and God said to them, 'Be fruitful and multiply, and fill the earth, and subdue it; and rule over the fish of the sea and over the birds of the sky and over every living thing that moves on the earth.'"*

Adam received the authority and power to manage and rule over all things from God. He was the lord of all things but after a long time, he and his wife were deceived into eating from the tree of the knowledge of good and evil by the crafty serpent. He committed a sin of disobedience to God.

It reads in Romans 6:16, *"Do you not know that when you present yourselves to someone as slaves for obedience, you are slaves of the one whom you obey, either of sin resulting in death, or of obedience resulting in righteousness?"* You are a slave to sin or righteousness. If you commit sins, you are a slave to sin and will be led to death. If you obey the Word of righteousness, however, you are a slave to righteousness and will enter heaven.

Adam committed a sin of disobedience to God and became a slave to sin. So he could no longer have all the authority and power that God had given him. He had to hand over the authority and power to the devil just as all possessions of a slave belong naturally to his master. In short, Adam handed over his authority and power that God had given him to the devil because he sinned and became a slave of sin.

Adam's disobedience resulted in sins of all men. It caused him and all his descendants to serve the devil as slaves and to be doomed to death.

The Law of the Redemption of the Land

What must people do to be set free from the enemy devil and Satan and be saved from sins and death? Some say, "God forgives everyone unconditionally because God is love. He abounds in compassion and mercy." However, 1 Corinthians 14:40 says, *"But all things must be done properly and in an orderly manner."* God does anything in an orderly manner according to the law of the spiritual realm. God does nothing against the spiritual law because He is the God of justice and fairness.

In the spiritual realm, there is a law to punish sinners, saying, "The wages of sin is death." Also, there is a law to redeem sinners. This spiritual law should be applied to recover the authority Adam had handed over to the devil.

Then, what is the law of the redemption of sinners? It is the law of the redemption of the land recorded in the Old Testament. Before the beginning of time, God the Father had prepared in secret the way of human salvation according to this law.

What Is the Law of the Redemption of the Land?

This is God's command to the Israelites in Leviticus 25:23-25:

> *The land, moreover, shall not be sold permanently, for the land is Mine; for you are but aliens and sojourners with Me. Thus for every piece of your property, you are to provide for the redemption of the land. If a fellow countryman of yours becomes so poor he has to sell part of his property, then his nearest kinsman is to come and buy back what his relative has sold.*

Every piece of land belongs to God and must not be sold permanently. If somebody sold his land because of his poverty, God allowed him or his nearest kinsman to buy back the land. This is the law of the redemption of the land.

People of Israel draw up the land contract certificate according to the law of the redemption of the land not to sell the land permanently, when they sell and buy the land.

The seller and buyer write down detailed contents of the land contract on the certificate so that the seller or his nearest kinsman can redeem it some time later. They make a copy of it and stamp both of their seals on the two contracts in front of two or three witnesses. One contract is sealed and kept in a warehouse of the holy temple. The other contract is kept in an entrance room, opened and unsealed. The law of the redemption of the land allows the seller and his nearest kinsman to redeem the land at any time.

The Law of the Redemption of the Land and Human Salvation

Why did God prepare the way of human salvation according to the law of the redemption of the land? Genesis 3:19 and 23 clearly tell us that the law of the redemption of the land has a direct connection with the salvation of mankind:

> *By the sweat of your face You will eat bread, till you return to the ground, because from it you were taken; for you are dust, and to dust you shall return* (Genesis 3:19).

> *The LORD God sent him out from the garden of Eden, to cultivate the ground from which he was taken* (Genesis 3:23).

God said to Adam after his disobedience, "For you are dust, and to dust you shall return." Here, "dust" symbolizes men who have been formed from dust. Therefore, men return to dust after death.

The law of the redemption of the land says that all lands are God's and must not be sold permanently (Leviticus 25:23-25). These verses mean that all men made from the dust of the land belong to God and cannot be sold permanently. It also indicates that no authorities and power Adam had received from God in the Garden of Eden could be sold permanently because they belonged to God.

Adam's authority was handed over to the enemy devil and Satan but he who is proper for redeeming Adam's lost authority could restore it from the enemy the devil. Likewise, the God of justice destined a perfect redeemer according to the law of the redemption of the land. That redeemer is the Savior of all men.

The Secret Hidden Since Before the Beginning of Time

Before time began, the God of love knew that Adam would disobey Him and all his descendants would fall into the way of death. He prepared the way of human salvation in secret and hid it until the time of His choosing arrived.

If the devil had known of God's way, it would have hindered God from resolving the sin and death of all men so that it would not lose its authority. 1 Corinthians 2:7 observes that *"But we speak God's wisdom in a mystery, the hidden wisdom which God predestined before the ages to our glory."*

Jesus Christ, the Wisdom of God

Romans 5:18-19 says, *"So then as through one transgression there resulted condemnation to all men, even so through one act of righteousness there resulted justification of life to all men. For as through the one man's disobedience the many were made sinners, even so through the obedience of the One the many will be made righteous."*

All men would become righteous and be saved through the obedience of one man just as all men became sinners and fell into the way of death because of the disobedience of one man.

Likewise, God sent Jesus Christ, whom He had prepared as the way of salvation in secret and let Jesus be crucified and raised again. From then on, whoever believes in Him is saved. In 1 Corinthians 1:18, God tells us that *"For the word of the cross is foolishness to those who are perishing, but to us who are being saved it is the power of God."*

It sounds foolish to some people that the Son of God the Almighty was insulted and killed by His creatures. However, this "foolish" plan of God is far wiser than the wisest human plans and God's "weakness" is far stronger than the greatest of human strength (1 Corinthians 1:19-24). The Bible explicitly says that no one can ever be made right in the sight of God by observing the Law. Yet, God opened the way of salvation to everyone who believes in Jesus Christ in this easy manner.

The wages of sin is death. Thus, nobody could be saved if Jesus had not died for our sins. Jesus was crucified for our sins and rose again by the power of God. Likewise, God prepared the way that might look weak or foolish and hid it for a long time.

God had hidden Jesus Christ and His crucifixion in secret because the enemy devil and Satan, if they had known of them, would hinder the way of human salvation. The devil would never have killed Jesus on the cross if he had known that God had prepared the way of salvation through the cross to redeem all men from sins, to save them from death, and to recover

Adam's authority from the devil.

Again, remember 1 Corinthians 2:7-8: *"But we speak God's wisdom in a mystery, the hidden wisdom which God predestined before the ages to our glory; the wisdom which none of the rulers of this age has understood; for if they had understood it they would not have crucified the Lord of glory."*

Jesus Is Qualified According to the Law

As every contract has regulations, the spiritual realm also has a rule, which dictates that the redeemer must be qualified to restore Adam's lost authority from the devil according to the law of the redemption of the land.

For example, suppose there is a man facing bankruptcy in his business. He has a big debt but has no ability to pay it off. If he has a wealthy brother who loves him, his brother will pay off all his debts at once.

All men who are sinners since Adam's fall need a redeemer who is qualified to cleanse them from sins. What, then, are the qualifications of the redeemer? Why does the Bible say only Jesus is qualified?

First, the Redeemer must be a man

In Leviticus 25:25, it says, *"If a fellow countryman of yours becomes so poor he has to sell part of his property, then his nearest kinsman is to come and buy back what his relative has sold.*" The law of the redemption of the land says that if a man becomes poor and sells his property his closest kinsman can redeem what he sells.

1 Corinthians 15:21-22 reads, *"For since by a man came death, by a man also came the resurrection of the dead. For as in Adam all die, so also in Christ all will be made alive."* The first qualification of the Redeemer who can restore Adam's authority is that he must be a man. This fact is described once again in detail in Revelation 5:1-5:

> *I saw in the right hand of Him who sat on the throne a book written inside and on the back, sealed up with seven seals. And I saw a strong angel proclaiming with a loud voice, "Who is worthy to open the book and to break its seals?" And no one in heaven or on the earth or under the earth was able to open the book or to look into it. Then I began to weep greatly because no one was found worthy to open the book or to look into it; and one of the elders said to me, "Stop weeping; behold, the Lion that is from the tribe of Judah, the Root of David, has overcome so as to open the book and its seven seals."*

"A book written inside and on the back, sealed up with seven seals" indicates a contract that had been made between God and the devil when Adam disobeyed God and became a sinner. The apostle John could not find anyone who was worthy of breaking the seals and opening the scroll in heaven or on earth, or under the earth.

It was because angels in heaven are not men, all men on earth are sinners as Adam's descendants, and under the earth, there are only evil spirits belonging to the devil and dead souls who are to fall into Hell.

At that time, one of the elders told John, "Stop weeping; behold, the Lion that is from the tribe of Judah, the Root of David, has overcome so as to open the book and its seven seals." Here, "the Root of David" refers to Jesus, who was born as a descendant of King David of the tribe of Judah (Acts 13:22-23). Therefore, Jesus is qualified for the first condition of the law of the redemption of the land.

Some may say that "God is the Absolute. Jesus is surely God because He is the Son of God. He is never a man." Remember, however, John 1:1 that reads *"The Word was God,"* and John 1:14, which reads *"And the Word became flesh, and dwelt among us."* God, who was the Word, became flesh and lived here on earth among us.

It was Jesus whose original entity was God and who became flesh like man. He was the Word in His entity and the Son of God. He had humanity and divinity. However, He was born and grew up in a human likeness in the flesh. The history of mankind is divided into two parts with the time of Jesus' birth as a divider: B.C., *Before Christ*, and A.D., *Anno Domini*. This alone testifies that Jesus became flesh and came down to this earth. The birth of Jesus, upbringing, and crucifixion are also parts of this obvious fact.

Jesus, therefore, is a man and qualified to be our Redeemer.

Second, He must not be Adam's descendant

A debtor cannot pay off other people's debt. He who has no debt and has ability to help others can pay it off. In the same way, the redeemer of all men must be blameless and spotless in order to redeem all men from sins and death. All people are Adam's descendants and sinners because the first forefather of all men Adam sinned. None of his descendants is qualified to be the redeemer of all men because they themselves are sinners. Even one of the greatest men in the history cannot be responsible for sins of others.

Does Jesus have this qualification?

Matthew 1:18-21 describes Jesus' birth. He was conceived by the Holy Spirit, not through the unification of a man and a woman. The verses read:

> *Now the birth of Jesus Christ was as follows: when His mother Mary had been betrothed to Joseph, before they came together she was found to be with child by the Holy Spirit. And Joseph her husband, being a righteous man and not wanting to disgrace her, planned to send her away secretly. But when he had considered this, behold, an angel of the Lord appeared to him in a dream, saying, "Joseph, son of David, do not be afraid to take Mary as your wife; for the Child who has been conceived in her is of the Holy Spirit. She will bear a Son; and you shall call His name Jesus, for He will save His people from their sins."*

Jesus was David's descendant according to His genealogy (Matthew 1:1-17; Luke 3:23-38). However, He was conceived by the Holy Spirit before Mary united with Joseph. Therefore, He had no sinful nature.

Everyone is born with the original sin because he inherits the sinful nature from his parents. In other words, after Adam sinned, he handed down his sinful nature to all his descendants. The sinful nature has been inherited to all men to this day, and that sin is called the "original sin." For this reason, all descendants of Adam are sinners and cannot redeem any other man.

Thus, God the Father planned His Son Jesus to be conceived by the Holy Spirit in the womb of the Virgin Mary. In this way, Jesus became flesh and came down to this world, but was not a descendant of Adam.

Third, He must have power to overcome the devil

Again, Leviticus 25:26-27 tells us:

> *Or in case a man has no kinsman, but so recovers his means as to find sufficient for its redemption, then he shall calculate the years since its sale and refund the balance to the man to whom he sold it, and so return to his property.*

In short, a redeemer should have the power to buy back the

sold land. A poor man cannot pay off the debt of his friend even if he desires to do so. In the same way, the redeemer must have no sin to be able to save all men from their sins. Having no sin is one's strength in the spiritual realm.

The Redeemer must have the power to defeat the enemy devil and Satan and to restore Adam's lost authority. That is, the Redeemer must have neither the original sin nor his own sin. Only a sinless redeemer can defeat the devil and liberate all men from the devil.

Was Jesus sinless?

Jesus had no original sin because He was conceived by the Holy Spirit. He obeyed the law of God fully because He grew up under the control of parents who feared God. He fulfilled the Law with love. He was circumcised on the eighth day after His birth (Luke 2:21). He never committed His own sin and only obeyed the will of God the Father until He was crucified at the age of thirty-three (1 Peter 2:22-24; Hebrews 7:26).

Jesus could defeat the devil and could redeem all men because He had no sin at all. His "sinlessness" was testified through His many works of power. He drove out demons, made the blind see, the deaf hear, the lame walk, and healed any kind of incurable diseases. A heavy storm calmed down and a fierce wind stopped when He rebuked the wind and said to the water, *"Hush, be still!"* (Mark 4:39)

Lastly, He must have a sacrificial love

Even a rich man would not redeem the land if he did not have love for the man who sold the land. In the same way, the redeemer must have love for sinners to the point of sacrificing Himself to resolve once and for all the problems of sins.

In Ruth 4:1-6, Boaz was well aware of Naomi's poverty and told her nearest kinsman—a redeemer to buy her land back if he wanted. Yet, the man refused, saying to Boaz, *"I cannot redeem it for myself, because I would jeopardize my own inheritance. Redeem it for yourself; you may have my right of redemption, for I cannot redeem it"* (v. 6). He did not redeem the land for Naomi and Ruth even though he was rich enough to do so. That was because he had no sacrificing love. After all, Boaz, the next nearest kinsman-redeemer, redeemed the land because he had such sacrificing love.

Boaz became a legal redeemer and married Ruth because he had enough love to redeem the land of Naomi. The son to whom Boaz and Ruth gave birth was the great grandfather of King David and was recorded in Jesus' family line.

Jesus was crucified in love. Jesus was the Word, but became flesh and came to this earth. He was not a descendant of Adam because he was conceived through the Holy Spirit. So He was born with no original sin. He had the power to redeem all men from sins because He was sinless.

However, He could not have become the Redeemer without a spiritual and sacrificing love even if He might have had other three qualifications. He had to take the penalty of sins that sinners were doomed to take up so that He would redeem all men from sins.

He had to be treated as the most serious and dangerous criminal and be hung on the rugged wooden cross. He had to be insulted and mocked, and shed all blood and water from His body to save all men. He had to pay a high price and make a great sacrifice.

You cannot find anywhere in human history an instance in which a blameless prince died for his evil and stupid people. Jesus is the only begotten Son of God the Almighty, the King of kings, the Lord of lords, and the Master of all creation. Such great, noble, and blameless Jesus was hung on the cross and died shedding His blood. How immeasurable a love did He have for us?

In fact, Jesus did only good deeds throughout His life. He gave sinners forgiveness, healed all kinds of sick people, released many people from demons, gave the good news of peace, joy, and love, and gave people a sincere hope for Heaven and salvation. Above all, He gave His own life for sinners.

Romans 5:7-8 reads, *"For one will hardly die for a righteous man; though perhaps for the good man someone would dare even to die. But God demonstrates His own love toward us, in that while we were yet sinners, Christ died for us."* God the Father sent His only begotten Son Jesus for us who are neither righteous nor good, and allowed Him to be hung on the cross and die on it. He demonstrated His great love in this way.

Therefore, I pray in the name of the Lord that you may understand that you cannot be saved in the name of anyone else except for Jesus Christ, gain the right to become a child of God by accepting Jesus Christ, and always enjoy triumphant life in the assurance of salvation!

Chapter 5

WHY IS JESUS OUR ONLY SAVIOR?

- The Providence of Salvation
  through Jesus Christ
- Why Was Jesus Hung
  on the Wooden Cross?
- No Other Name in the World
  but "Jesus Christ"

"He is the stone which was rejected by you, the builders, but which became the chief corner stone. And there is salvation in no one else; for there is no other name under heaven that has been given among men by which we must be saved."

Acts 4:11-12

You will love God with all your heart when you realize His deep and attentive providence of the human cultivation. Moreover, you must admire His love and wisdom when you realize the providence of salvation through Jesus Christ.

Then, how was the providence of salvation that had been hidden before the time began accomplished through Jesus Christ? I told you earlier that the God of justice had prepared the one who was qualified for redeeming all people according to the spiritual law and that there is no one else but Jesus under heaven who meets that qualification.

Jesus is the only one who was a man but not a descendant of Adam because He was conceived by the Holy Spirit and came to the earth in flesh. In addition, He had the power and love to redeem all people. So He could open the way of salvation to all human beings by being crucified.

Therefore, it is said in Acts 4:12, *"And there is salvation in no one else; for there is no other name under heaven that has been given among men by which we must be saved."* Whoever accepts and believes in Jesus Christ is forgiven of all sins and saved. He will come out to the light from the darkness and receive the authority and blessings of children of God.

Now, I will explain why you must believe in Jesus who was crucified in order for you to be saved and receive the authority and blessings of a child of God.

The Providence of Salvation through Jesus Christ

God prepared the way of salvation before time began. The Book of Genesis prophesied about Jesus and the secret of human salvation through the cross.

Genesis 3:14-15 reads:

> *The LORD God said to the serpent, "Because you have done this, cursed are you more than all cattle, and more than every beast of the field; on your belly you will go, and dust you will eat all the days of your life; and I will put enmity between you and the woman, and between your seed and her seed; He shall bruise you on the head, and you shall bruise him on the heel."*

As discussed before, spiritually, the "serpent" refers to the enemy devil and "eating dust" symbolizes the enemy devil reigning men who were made from the dust of the ground. Also, "woman" indicates "Israel" and "the seed of the woman" refers to Jesus. The phrase "You [the serpent] shall bruise him on the heel" symbolizes that Jesus will be crucified, and "he [the seed of the woman] will bruise him [the serpent] on the head" implies that Jesus would break the camp of the enemy devil and Satan by resurrecting from the dead.

Satan Could Not Realize God's Plan

God had hidden this providence of salvation in secret, so the enemy devil and Satan could not know and grasp His wisdom.

The enemy devil and Satan tried to kill the offspring of the woman before being crushed. He thought that he could forever have the authority that had been handed over from Adam, who had disobeyed God. However, the enemy devil and Satan did not know who the offspring of the woman was. Thus, he tried to kill the prophets who were loved by God from the time of the Old Testament.

When Moses was born, the enemy devil and Satan had Pharaoh, the king of Egypt, kill every boy born of Hebrew women (Exodus 1:15-22). When Jesus was conceived by the Holy Spirit and came to the earth in flesh, the enemy devil and Satan had King Herod do the same.

However, God had already known the plan of the enemy Satan. The angel of the Lord appeared in Joseph's dream and told him to go to Egypt with the baby and mother. God allowed the family to live there until King Herod died.

Jesus' Crucifixion Permitted by God

Jesus grew up in the protection of God and began His ministry from the age of thirty. He went throughout Galilee, teaching in the synagogues, healing all manner of sickness and all manner of disease among the people, raising the dead up, and preaching the gospel to the poor (Matthew 4:23, 11:5).

Meanwhile, the enemy devil and Satan schemed again to have the chief priests, scribes, and the Pharisees kill Jesus. However, as you know through the Bible, an evil man could not even touch Jesus because all events during His life took place in the providence of God.

God allowed the enemy devil and Satan to crucify Jesus only after three years of His ministry. As a result, Jesus wore a crown of thorns and died on the cross suffering great pain of being nailed on His hands and feet.

Crucifixion is the cruelest way of execution. The enemy devil was greatly pleased after he killed Jesus in this cruel way. Satan sang for joy of victory because he thought he would keep reigning over the world, as there would be no one who could thwart his regime. Yet, there was the hidden secret providence of God.

The Enemy Devil and Satan Broke the Spiritual Law

God does not use His absolute sovereign power against the law because He is righteous. He prepared the way of salvation by the spiritual law before time began, for He performs everything by the spiritual law.

Since the wages of sin is death according to the spiritual law (Romans 6:23), no one faces his death if he has no sin. However, the enemy devil and Satan crucified Jesus who was blameless and unblemished (1 Peter 2:22-23). By doing this, the enemy devil broke the spiritual law and was deceived by his own trick. He became an instrument for human salvation that had been planned by God. The offspring of the woman crushed his head as prophesied in Genesis.

Generally, a serpent can still resist even if you step on its tail or cut its body off, but it cannot resist if you hold its head tight. Therefore, the phrase, "And I will put enmity between you and the woman, and between your seed and her seed; he shall bruise you on the head, and you shall bruise him on the heel" spiritually means that the enemy Satan will lose his power and authority due to Jesus Christ. The serpent striking the heel of the offspring of the woman spiritually means that Satan will crucify Jesus, and this was fulfilled as it was foretold in Genesis 3:15.

Salvation through Jesus' Crucifixion

The way of salvation that had been hidden by God before time began was fulfilled when Jesus resurrected on the third day of His crucifixion.

About 6,000 years ago, Adam had to hand over his authority given from God to the enemy devil as he broke the law of the spiritual realm by his disobedience (Luke 4:6). However, after 4,000 years, Satan had to go to the way of destruction by breaking the spiritual law.

Therefore, the enemy devil had to set free those who accepted Jesus as their Savior and believed in His name, and they came to receive the right to become children of God. Would the enemy devil have crucified Jesus if he had known this wisdom of God? Not at all! In 1 Corinthians 2:8, we are reminded that

"The wisdom which none of the rulers of this age has understood; for if they had understood it they would not have crucified the Lord of glory."

Those who do not understand this fact nowadays also wonder, "Why could God the Almighty not protect His Son from death? Why did He let Him die on the cross?" However, if you thoroughly understood the providence of the cross, you would know why Jesus had to be crucified and how He could become the King of kings and the Lord of lords after His triumphant victory over the enemy the devil. Thus, whoever believes Jesus as the Savior who died on the cross and resurrected three days later to redeem men from all sins can be declared righteous and be saved.

Why Was Jesus Hung on the Wooden Cross?

Why then, should Jesus be hung on a wooden cross? Why should it be a wooden cross? Among a variety of methods of execution, Jesus died on the wooden cross. According to Galatians 3:13-14, there are three spiritual reasons why Jesus was hung on a wooden cross.

First, to Redeem Us from the Curse of the Law

Galatians 3:13 reads, *"Christ redeemed us from the curse of the Law, having become a curse for us for it is written,*

'Cursed is everyone who hangs on a tree.'" It explains that Jesus redeemed us from the curse of the Law by being hung on a wooden cross.

All men were cursed and thus destined to go to the way of death because of the first man Adam's disobedience as written in Romans 6:23, *"the wages of sin is death."* However, God gave His Son Jesus for humanity and allowed Him to be hung on a wooden cross to redeem them from the curse of the Law (Deuteronomy 21:23).

Furthermore, Jesus shed His precious blood on the cross. Observe Verses 11 and 14 from Leviticus 17:

> *For the life of the flesh is in the blood, and I have given it to you on the altar to make atonement for your souls; for it is the blood by reason of the life that makes atonement* (v. 11).

> *For as for the life of all flesh, its blood is identified with its life....* (v. 14).

The author of Leviticus writes that the life is blood because every creature needs blood in order to live and would die without it.

However, when one dies, his flesh goes back to dust, and his soul will go to either Heaven or Hell. To receive eternal life, you must be forgiven of all your sins. To be forgiven of your sins, there must be the shedding of blood as dictated in Hebrews 9:22, *"And according to the Law, one may almost say all things are cleansed with blood, and without shedding of blood there is no forgiveness."* For this reason, people during Old Testament days had to offer the blood of animals whenever they sinned. Yet, Jesus shed His precious blood once and for all to make people be forgiven and receive eternal life because He Himself had neither the original sin nor self-committed sin.

Likewise, you can receive eternal life because of Jesus' precious blood. That is, Jesus died in your place and opened the way for you to be a child of God.

Second, to Give Abraham's Blessing

The first half of Galatians 3:14 says that *"In order that in Christ Jesus the blessing of Abraham might come to the Gentiles."* This means that God gives the blessing given to Abraham not only to the Israelites but also to all the Gentiles who are declared righteous by accepting Jesus as their Savior.

Abraham was called as the "father of faith" and "God's friend," and he lived in the blessings of children, health, long-life, wealth and so on. The reason Abraham was abundantly blessed is written in Genesis 22:15-18:

> *Then the angel of the LORD called to Abraham a second time from heaven, and said, "By Myself I have sworn, declares the LORD, because you have done this thing and have not withheld your son, your only son, indeed I will greatly bless you, and I will greatly multiply your seed as the stars of the heavens and as the*

sand which is on the seashore; and your seed shall possess the gate of their enemies. In your seed all the nations of the earth shall be blessed, because you have obeyed My voice."

Abraham obeyed when God told him to *"Go forth from your country, and from your relatives and from your father's house, to the land which I will show you"* (Genesis 12:1). He also obeyed without any excuse or complaints when God said, *"Take now your son, your only son, whom you love, Isaac, and go to the land of Moriah, and offer him there as a burnt offering on one of the mountains of which I will tell you"* (Genssis 22:2). This was possible for Abraham because he believed God who could revive the dead (Hebrews 11:19). He was able to be a blessing and the father of faith as he had such a firm faith.

Therefore, God's children who accept Jesus as their Savior should have the faith of Abraham. You will then be able to give glory to God by receiving all blessings of the earth.

Third, to Give the Promise of the Spirit

The second half of Galatians 3:14 reads, *"So that we would receive the promise of the Spirit through faith."* This means that anyone who believes that Jesus died on the wooden cross for all human beings is released from the curse of the Law and receives the promise of the Holy Spirit. In addition, whoever accepts Jesus as the Savior receives the authority of a child of God and the Holy Spirit as a gift and assurance (John 1:12;

Romans 8:16).

When you receive the Holy Spirit, you can call God "Abba, Father" (Romans 8:15), your name is written on the Book of Life in heaven (Luke 10:20), and you have the citizenship of heaven (Philippians 3:20). This is because the Holy Spirit, which is the heart and strength of God, leads you to the eternal life by helping you to understand the Word of God and to live according to His Word with faith.

However, you will be saved when you not only acknowledge Jesus as your Savior but also believe in your heart that He broke the authority of death and resurrected. Romans 10:9 concerns this: *"If you confess with your mouth Jesus as Lord, and believe in your heart that God raised Him from the dead, you will be saved."*

Before the beginning of time, God destined the great plan to make those who would believe Jesus as the Savior become united with God and lead them to salvation. The plan is very wonderful and mysterious. Human beings had to go to the way of death because of the first man's sin according to the law of the spiritual realm, which claims that "The wages of sin is death." However, they could be set free from the curse of the Law and saved in faith by the same law because of Satan's violation of the law of the spiritual realm.

Human beings had to suffer from pain, troubles, and death that the enemy the devil brought when they became slaves to the sins because of the disobedience. However, whoever accepts Jesus as the Savior and receives the Holy Spirit can gain the salvation, eternal life, resurrection, and overflowing blessings.

The Privilege and Blessing Given to the Children of God

Whoever opens his heart and accepts Jesus Christ is forgiven, receives the right to become a child of God, and enjoys peace and joy in his heart. This is possible because Jesus took all our sins once and for all by being crucified. So, it is said in Psalm 103:12, *"As far as the east is from the west, so far has He removed our transgressions from us."* Also, it reads in Hebrews 10:16-18 that *"'This is the covenant that I will make with them after those days,' says the Lord: 'I will put My laws upon their heart, and on their mind I will write them,' He then says, 'And their sins and their lawless deeds I will remember no more.' Now where there is forgiveness of these things, there is no longer any offering for sin."*

There is nothing in the world that deserves to be compared to the right of children of God given by faith. In this world, the right of children of a king or a president is very powerful. How great, then, is the right of children of God the Creator who rules over the world and governs the human history and the universe?

God does not consider it as true faith when you only claim, "Jesus is the Savior." You should understand who Jesus Christ is, why He is the only Savior for you, and have true faith on the basis of that knowledge. Then, with that true faith, you can realize the providence of God hidden in the cross and confess, "The Lord is the Christ and the Son of the living God." Furthermore, you can live according to the will of God. Without this true faith, it is very difficult for you to have the faith coming from the heart and live according to the Word of God.

Therefore, as written in Matthew 7:21, *"Not everyone who says to Me, 'Lord, Lord,' will enter the kingdom of heaven, but he who does the will of My Father who is in heaven will enter,"* Jesus explicitly declared that only the people who claim to Jesus "Lord, Lord" and live by the will and Word of God would be saved.

No Other Name in the World but "Jesus Christ"

Acts 4 portrays a scene in which Peter and John boldly testifies the name of Jesus Christ before the Sanhedrin. They sincerely believed that there was no other name beside "Jesus Christ" through which man could reach salvation, and Peter, who was filled with the Holy Spirit, was empowered to proclaim that *"And there is salvation in no one else; for there is no other name under heaven that has been given among men by which we must be saved"* (v. 12).

What spiritual implications are there in the name "Jesus Christ"? And why has God given us no other name but Jesus Christ by which we must reach salvation?

The Difference between "Jesus" and "Jesus Christ"

Acts 16:31 tells us to *"Believe in the Lord Jesus, and you will be saved, you and your household."* There is an important reason why it reads "the Lord Jesus," not simply "Jesus."

Here, "Jesus" refers to a man who will save His people from their sins. "Christ" is a Greek word that means "Messiah" in Hebrew. It is "the one who was anointed" and it refers to the Savior who is the Mediator between God and men. That is, "Jesus" is the name of the future savior, but "Christ" is the name of the Savior who has already saved people.

During Old Testament days, God anointed the person who would be a king, or a priest, or a prophet by pouring oil over the anointed-to-be's head (Leviticus 4:3; 1 Samuel 10:1; 1 Kings 19:16). Oil symbolizes the Holy Spirit. Therefore, to anoint someone means to give the Holy Spirit to the person elected by God.

Jesus was anointed as the King, the Chief Priest, and the Prophet, and came to this world in flesh to save all human beings according to the providence of God that had been destined before the beginning of time. He was crucified to redeem us, and became our Savior by resurrecting on the third day. Accordingly, He is the Savior who has completed God's providence of salvation. That is, He is the Christ.

Of the pre-crucifixion Jesus, we refer to Him only as "Jesus." However, after crucifixion and resurrection, He is to be addressed as "Jesus Christ," "the Lord Jesus," or "the Lord."

You should know that there is a great difference of power between "Jesus" and "Jesus Christ." Jesus is the name by which He was called before He fulfilled the providence of salvation and the enemy devil is not afraid of this name as much. The name "Jesus Christ," however, implies the following three: the blood that redeemed us from our sins; resurrection that broke the authority of death; and life that is everlasting. Before this name, however, the enemy devil trembles in fear.

Many people neglect this fact because they do not understand this difference. However, it is true that God's work and answer would be different by which name you call (Acts 3:6).

When you pray to God in the name of our Lord Jesus Christ and keep this fact in mind, you would lead a victorious life filled with prompt and abundant answers from your God the Almighty.

Jesus' Complete Obedience

Though Jesus was God in the very nature, He did not consider equality with God something to be grasped, nor clang to His rights as God. He made Himself nothing; He took the humble position of a slave and appeared in the form of a human being.

A good servant does not have his own will. He works according to the will of his master instead of his own. It is the duty of a servant to obey the will of his master whether or not it is in accordance with his own will or feeling. Jesus obeyed God's will with the heart of a good servant, and thus could accomplish His mission for human salvation.

God exalted Jesus, who obeyed the will of God, saying, "Yes" and "Amen," to the highest place and let many people confess that He is the Lord.

For this reason also, God highly exalted Him, and

bestowed on Him the name which is above every name, so that at the name of Jesus every knee will bow, of those who are in heaven and on earth and under the earth, and that every tongue will confess that Jesus Christ is Lord, to the glory of God the Father (Philippians 2:9-11).

The Name "Lord Jesus" Testifies God's Power

It says in John 1:3, *"All things came into being through Him, and apart from Him nothing came into being that has come into being."* As all things in the world were created through Jesus, He has the authority to rule over all things as the Creator. When Jesus the Son of God the Creator commanded, lifeless things such as a stormy wind and wave obeyed Him and calmed down, and a fig tree withered immediately when He cursed it.

Jesus had the authority to forgive sins and save sinners from the punishment of their sins. So, Jesus said to a paralytic in Matthew 9:2, *"Take courage, son; your sins are forgiven"* and said in verse 6, *"'But so that you may know that the Son of Man has authority on earth to forgive sins.' Then He said to the paralytic, 'Get up, pick up your bed and go home.'"*

In addition, Jesus had the power to heal all kinds of diseases and disabilities, and revive the dead. John 11 describes a scene in which the dead man Lazarus came out from the tomb with his hands and feet wrapped with strips of linen when Jesus called in a loud voice, "Lazarus, come out". He had been dead for four days and there was a bad odor, but he walked out of the tomb as a healthy man.

Likewise, Jesus gives you whatever you ask with faith because He has the wonderful power of God.

Jesus Christ, the Love of God

As it says in 1 John 4:10, *"In this is love, not that we loved God, but that He loved us and sent His Son to be the propitiation for our sins,"* God showed His amazing love to us. He sent His only begotten Son as an atoning sacrifice when we were still sinners. God had to endure great pain and opened the way of human salvation when His Son Jesus was nailed on the cross and shed the blood. How did the God of love feel when He had to see His only begotten Son Jesus crucified? God was not able to watch sitting on His throne. Matthew 27:51-54 tells us how much God suffered when Jesus was crucified.

> *And behold, the veil of the temple was torn in two from top to bottom; and the earth shook and the rocks were split. The tombs were opened, and many bodies of the saints who had fallen asleep were raised; and coming out of the tombs after His resurrection they entered the holy city and appeared to many. Now the centurion, and those who were with him keeping guard over Jesus, when they saw the earthquake and the things that were happening, became very frightened and said, "Truly this was the Son of God!"*

This shows clearly that Jesus was crucified not because of His own sins but because of the great love of God to lead all men to the way of salvation. However, so many people do not accept or understand this amazing love of God.

After Adam's disobedience, human beings could not be with God and became men of the sinful nature. However, Jesus came to the earth and became the Mediator between God and us so that He might give the blessings of Immanuel to all men (Matthew 1:23). Through Jesus' pain and sufferings on the cross, we gain true peace and rest.

Therefore, I hope you understand the great love of God who gave us His only Son as a ransom to redeem us from sins and eternal death, and the sacrificial love of the Lord who, even though He was blameless, was crucified on our behalf and opened the way of salvation.

Chapter 6

THE PROVIDENCE OF THE CROSS

- Born in a Stable and Laid in a Manger
- Jesus' Life in Poverty
- Whipped and Shedding His Blood
- Wearing the Crown of Thorns
- Jesus' Garments and Tunic
- Nailed through His Hands and Feet
- Jesus' Legs Not Broken but His Side Pierced

"Surely our griefs He Himself bore, and our sorrows He carried; yet we ourselves esteemed Him stricken, smitten of God, and afflicted. But He was pierced through for our transgressions, He was crushed for our iniquities; the chastening for our well-being fell upon Him, and by His scourging we are healed. All of us like sheep have gone astray, each of us has turned to his own way; but the LORD has caused the iniquity of us all to fall on Him."

Isaiah 53:4-6

In God's plan for obtaining true children, the most important part is that Jesus came in flesh to this world, was afflicted with all kinds of suffering, and died on the cross. Through all this, He accomplished the way for the salvation of human beings.

God's providence of the cross has a deep spiritual meaning. Jesus, the only begotten Son of God, forsaking the heavenly glory, was born in a pen of animals, and lived in poverty throughout His life.

In addition, He was whipped and nailed on His hands and feet, wore a crown of thorns and shed blood and water by having His side pierced with a spear. Every suffering Jesus experienced contains the overwhelming love of God.

When you fully understand the spiritual meaning of the cross and Jesus' sufferings, your heart will surely be moved at the love of God and you will have true faith. You can also receive answers to all troubles in your life such as poverty and disease, as well as the everlasting kingdom of heaven.

Born in a Stable and Laid in a Manger

Jesus, being in very nature God, was the master of all things in heaven and on earth and the most glorious being.

Nevertheless, He came in flesh to this world in order to redeem human beings from sin and lead them to salvation.

Jesus is the only begotten Son of God the Almighty Creator. Why, then, was He not born in a luxurious place or at least in a cozy room? Could God not have let Him be born in a gorgeous place? Why did He have Jesus born in a stable and laid in a manger?

There is a deep spiritual meaning in this. You should know that Jesus was born spiritually in the most glorious manner. Even though people could not see with their physical eyes, God was so pleased with the birth of Jesus that He circled the baby Jesus with lights of glory in the presence of a great company of heavenly host and angels. You can feel a sense of His excitement from Luke 2:14, which records the following: *"Glory to God in the highest, and on earth peace among men with whom He is pleased."* God had also prepared good shepherds and the Magi from the East and led them to worship the baby Jesus.

All the praise and worship took place because Jesus would open the door of salvation with His coming to this world, a great multitude of people would enter the eternal heaven as children of God, and Jesus the Son of God would be the King of kings and the Lord of lords.

God's Providence Hidden in the Birth of Jesus

When Jesus was born, Caesar Augustus issued a decree that a census be taken of the entire Roman Empire. The Jewish people were under the colonial rule of the Rome and went back to their hometowns to register, heeding the command of Caesar.

Joseph also went up with his fiancée Mary from the town of Nazareth in Galilee to Bethlehem the town of David, because he belonged to the house and line of David. Mary was pledged to Joseph and conceived a child by the Holy Spirit before they went there, and gave birth to the firstborn Jesus during their stay there.

The name "Bethlehem" means "House of Bread," and it was the hometown of King David (1 Samuel 16:1). Micah 5:2 writes of the town of Bethlehem as follows: *"But as for you, Bethlehem Ephrathah, too little to be among the clans of Judah, from you One will go forth for Me to be ruler in Israel. His goings forth are from long ago, from the days of eternity."* Bethlehem was prophesied as the birthplace of the Messiah.

At that time there was no room for Mary and Joseph in any inn, because thousands of people were in Bethlehem to register. There, Mary gave birth to a baby in a stable. She wrapped Him in swaddling cloths and placed Him in a manger, a long container used to feed cows or horses.

Then, why was Jesus, who came as the Savior of human beings, born in such a lowly and humble manner?

To Redeem Animal-like Men

Ecclesiastes 3:18 reads, *"I said to myself concerning the sons of men, 'God has surely tested them in order for them to see that they are but beasts.'"* Men, who have lost the image of God, are like the animals in the sight of God. The first man

Adam was originally a living being created in the image of God. He was also a man of spirit because God taught him only the Word of truth.

However, Adam ate the fruit of the tree of the knowledge of good and evil against the command of God, so his spirit died and he could not communicate with God anymore. In addition, he was no longer the lord of all creation. Satan instigated Adam to follow the sinful nature, and his pure and truthful heart changed into an impure and untruthful heart.

In your daily life, you may sometimes have heard an expression "He is no better than an animal." You often hear about people who are no better than animals through the media. For their own benefits, they easily deceive and cheat their neighbors, customers, friends, and family members. Parents and children hate and sometimes seem ready to kill each other.

People dare to do such evil deeds because soul has become the master of man since the death of spirit, and they have lost the image of God because of their sins. Like animals that are only made of soul and body, such people cannot enter heaven nor can call God Abba Father. Jesus was born in a stable to redeem human beings who are no better than animals.

Jesus Is True Spiritual Food

Jesus was laid in a manger, a feed container for horses, in order to be true spiritual food for human beings who are no better than animals (John 6:51).

In other words, it was divine providence to lead man to the

complete salvation by enabling him to recover the lost image of God and perform the whole duty of man. What, then, is the whole duty of man? Ecclesiastes 12:13-14 provides us with some insights:

> *The conclusion, when all has been heard, is: fear God and keep His commandments, because this applies to every person. For God will bring every act to judgment, everything which is hidden, whether it is good or evil.*

What does "fearing God" mean? Proverbs 8:13 tells us that *"The fear of the LORD is to hate evil."* Therefore, to fear God is not to accept evil any more and at the same time to throw away any kind of evil from inside your heart.

If you really fear God, you should do your best to discard any kind of evil, and struggle against sin and cast it off to the point of shedding blood. Like students studying hard to ensure a better future, you should do your best to fear God and do the whole duty of man to enjoy God's love and blessing.

In the Bible, you can find God's commands given to His children like "do this; don't do that; keep this; and cast that off." On the one hand, God tells us that what the children of God ought to do is "pray, love, give thanks and many more." On the other hand, God commands us not to do things leading to death such as hatred, adultery and drunkenness.

He also tells us to obey certain commands, such as "Keep the Sabbath day holy," "Keep your promises," and the like. God also urges us to discard something harmful, saying, "Avoid every kind of evil," "Throw away your greed," and so forth.

It is the whole duty of man to fear God and keep His commands. God will hold us accountable for each of our deeds on the Judgment Day, every hidden thing whether it is good or evil. Thus, when you live like an animal without carrying out the whole duty of man, it is natural for you to fall into Hell as a result of the judgment of God.

Likewise, Jesus was born in a stable and was laid in a manger to redeem men who are no better than animals and to become true spiritual food for them.

Jesus' Life in Poverty

John 3:35 says, *"The Father loves the Son and has given all things into His hand."* You read in Colossians 1:16, *"For by Him all things were created, both in the heavens and on earth, visible and invisible, whether thrones or dominions or rulers or authorities all things have been created through Him and for Him."* In other words, Jesus is the only Son of God the Creator, and the Lord of all things in heaven and on earth.

Why, then, did He come to this world in a very lowly and humble state and live in poverty though He was in very nature God the Almighty and was by every measure rich?

To Redeem Men From Poverty

2 Corinthians 8:9 reads, *"For you know the grace of our*

Lord Jesus Christ, that though He was rich, yet for your sake He became poor, so that you through His poverty might become rich." The providence of the amazing love of God is manifested in this. Jesus, though he was the King of kings, the Lord of lords, and the only Son of God the Creator, forsook all the heavenly glory, came to this world, and lived in poverty enduring the disdain and maltreatment of people to redeem human beings from poverty.

In the beginning, God created man to take and eat fruits without sweat and to enjoy a prosperous life without difficult toil. However, after the first man Adam disobeyed the Word of God and corrupted, man could eat his food only through painful toil by the sweat of his brow. Because of this, man often lives in want and poverty.

Poverty itself is not a sin, so Jesus did not shed His blood to redeem us from poverty. Yet, poverty is a curse manifested after Adam's disobedience to God, thus Jesus made you rich by living in poverty.

Some say that Jesus' life-long poverty means spiritual poverty. However, because Jesus was conceived through the Holy Spirit and is one with God the Father, it is not right to think that He was spiritually poor.

You should keep in mind the fact that Jesus lived in poverty to redeem you from poverty and you can lead an abundant life with thanksgiving for the love and grace of God.

Some say that it is wrong to seek money in prayer. Others think that if you are a Christian, you should live in poverty. Yet, that is absolutely not the will of God.

In the Bible, you can read many words of blessing. For instance, you read in Deuteronomy 28:2-6 that:

All these blessings will come upon you and overtake you if you obey the LORD your God: Blessed shall you be in the city, and blessed shall you be in the country. Blessed shall be the offspring of your body and the produce of your ground and the offspring of your beasts, the increase of your herd and the young of your flock. Blessed shall be your basket and your kneading bowl. Blessed shall you be when you come in, and blessed shall you be when you go out.

3 John 1:2 urges us, *"Beloved, I pray that in all respects you may prosper and be in good health, just as your soul prospers."* In fact, God's chosen men such as Abraham, Isaac, Jacob, Joseph, and Daniel all led very prosperous lives.

To Lead a Rich Life

In His righteousness, God makes you reap what you sow. As parents want to give only the good things to their children, your loving God wants to give whatever you ask for in faith (Mark 11:24).

God wants to give you answers and blessings, but you cannot receive anything if you do not ask or when you ask without any discernment. Thus, if you try to reap something without sowing anything, you are mocking God and going against the spiritual law.

Some may say, "I want to sow, but I cannot because I am so poor." However, in the Bible, you can find many people who were very poor but did their best to sow and were richly blessed as a reward.

In 1 Kings 17, we find that there was a three-and-a-half-year famine in the land. While there was still a famine, a widow in Zarephath of Sidon made a small cake of bread for the prophet Elijah with a handful of flour in a jar and a little oil in a jug that were all she had. God was so pleased with her serving His servant and blessed her abundantly: the jar of flour was not used up and the jug of oil was not to run dry until the day God would give rain on the land (1 Kings 17:14).

On one occasion during Jesus' time, a poor widow put in two very small coins, worth only a fraction of a penny, into the temple treasury. Nevertheless, Jesus commended her, saying that the poor widow put in more than all the others. This was because she gave out of her poverty and put in everything—all that she had, while others gave a proportion of their possession (Mark 12:42-44).

The most important thing is your mindset to give everything to God. God does not see the quantity of your offering but smells the pleasing aroma of love and faith contained in the offering and plentifully blesses you.

Whipped and Shedding His Blood

Before the crucifixion, Roman soldiers mocked and disdained Jesus by slapping Him on His face, spitting on Him, and so on. They also flogged Jesus with a whip, a long leather strap with hooked pieces of lead dangling on it.

In those days, Roman soldiers were of the most robust, well disciplined, and the strongest forces in the world. How severe would the pain have been when they took off His clothes and whipped Him? When they lashed His body with the whip, His flesh was torn, the bones were exposed and blood gushed out.

To fulfill the prophecy of Isaiah *"I gave My back to those who strike Me, and My cheeks to those who pluck out the beard; I did not cover My face from humiliation and spitting"* (Isaiah 50:6), Jesus never attempted to avoid any of the whippings.

To Heal the Sickness and Illness

Why, then, was Jesus beaten with a whip and why did He shed His blood? Why did God permit this to occur to His Son? Isaiah 53 explains the purpose of Jesus' sufferings and affliction.

> *But He was pierced through for our transgressions, He was crushed for our iniquities; the chastening for our well-being fell upon Him, and by His scourging we are healed. All of us like sheep have gone astray, each of us has turned to his own way; but the LORD has caused*

the iniquity of us all to fall on Him (Isaiah 53:5-6).

Jesus was pierced and crushed for your transgressions and iniquities. He was punished, whipped and bled to give you peace and set you free from all diseases.

In Matthew 9, when Jesus healed a paralytic lying on a mat, He first solved his problem of sin, saying, "Your sins are forgiven." Only then, did Jesus tell him to "Get up, pick up your bed and go home."

In John 5, after Jesus healed one who had been an invalid for thirty-eight years, He said to him, *"Behold, you have become well; do not sin anymore, so that nothing worse happens to you"* (John 5:14).

The Bible tells you that diseases come upon you because of your sin. So you need someone who can solve your problem of sins, to be free from diseases. Without shedding of blood, however, there can be no forgiveness (Leviticus 17:11).

That is why, during Old Testament times, when someone committed sin, the priest slaughtered an animal as an atoning sacrifice. However, you are no longer in need of slaughtering animals as your offering after Jesus came in flesh to this world and shed His unblemished, spotless, and powerful blood. The holy blood of Jesus atoned for all sins of human beings in the past, the present, or even the future.

To Take Up Our Infirmities and Diseases

Matthew 8:17 reads, *"This was to fulfill what was spoken*

through Isaiah the prophet: 'He Himself took our infirmities and carried away our diseases.'" Thus, if you know why Jesus was flogged and shed His blood, and believe in it, you do not need to suffer from infirmities and diseases.

1 Peter 2:24 reads, "He Himself bore our sins in His body on the cross, so that we might die to sin and live to righteousness; for by His wounds you were healed." The present perfect tense is used in this verse because Jesus has already redeemed all the sins of human beings.

Regardless of claiming to believe the fact that Jesus bore our infirmities and diseases by His being lashed and bleeding, why do some of us still suffer from diseases?

God says in Exodus 15:26, "If you will give earnest heed to the voice of the LORD your God, and do what is right in His sight, and give ear to His commandments, and keep all His statutes, I will put none of the diseases on you which I have put on the Egyptians; for I, the LORD, am your healer." This means that if you do what is right in the sight of God, no disease will afflict you, because God with His eyes like a blazing fire protects you from them.

Let us take an example. When a child comes home crying after being beaten by a neighbor's child, parents' response and attitude toward this incident can be very different depending on their faith.

One may teach his child like this: "Why do you always get beaten up? If you are beaten once, you had better strike him back two or three times." Another parent may visit the parent of the child who beat his child and complain to them. Some other parent does not handle it in either way, but he may be very annoyed or indignant in his heart.

However, God tells you to overcome evil with goodness, love even your enemies, and seek peace with anyone, saying, *"But I say to you, do not resist an evil person; but whoever slaps you on your right cheek, turn the other to him also"* (Matthew 5:39).

Therefore, if you do what is right in His sight, it is not difficult for you to keep God's commandments and decrees. When you keep on praying and doing your best, God's grace and power come upon you and you can easily do anything with the help of the Holy Spirit.

If you discard sins and do what is right in God's sight, diseases cannot come upon you. Even if diseases do come upon you, God the Healer forgives your sins and heals you completely when you try to find out what is wrong in God's sight and repent of it with your whole heart.

Even though you confess with your lips that God is almighty if you rely on the world or go to a hospital when faced with a problem or an illness, God is not pleased with you because this proves that you do not truly believe in the Almighty God (2 Chronicles 16).

Wearing the Crown of Thorns

A crown is actually for a king with his royal robe. Although Jesus was the only begotten Son of God, the King of kings and the Lord of lords, He wore a crown made of long and hard thorns instead of a beautiful crown made of gold, silver, and jewels.

> *Then the soldiers of the governor took Jesus into the Praetorium and gathered the whole Roman cohort around Him. They stripped Him and put a scarlet robe on Him. And after twisting together a crown of thorns, they put it on His head, and a reed in His right hand; and they knelt down before Him and mocked Him, saying, "Hail, King of the Jews!" They spat on Him, and took the reed and began to beat Him on the head* (Matthew 27:27-30).

Roman soldiers twisted thorns together to create a crown too small for Jesus, and put it firmly on His head. So the thorns pierced His head and forehead, and blood flowed down His face. Why did God the Almighty allow His only begotten Son to wear a crown of thorns, suffer from a punishing pain, and shed His blood?

First, Jesus wore the crown of thorns to redeem us from the sins we commit in thought.

When man, created by God, communicated with Him and obeyed His Word, he did not commit a sin because he always thought in accordance with God's will and obeyed Him.

However, once he was tempted by the serpent and received the thought given by Satan, he soon committed a sin. He never thought of eating the fruit of the tree of the knowledge of good and evil before. After being tempted, however, he ate it because it seemed to be good for food and pleasing to the eye and also desirable for gaining wisdom.

Likewise, Satan, who led the first man Adam and Eve to disobey God, is working now to lead you to commit sins in thought.

In the human brain, there are cells responsible for memory. Ever since birth, what you have seen, heard, and learned were put in the memory cells with your own feelings to specific events, individuals, and information. We call this "knowledge." What we call "thought" is a process of the reproduction of this stored knowledge through the work of your soul.

People have grown up in different environments. What they have seen, heard, and learned is different from that of each other and what has been put in their brain is also different. Even if what they have seen, heard, and learned is the same, each one had his own feelings at the time and thus, it is inevitable that people have different values.

The Word of God is often not in accordance with our own knowledge and theory. For example, you may think that if you want to be exalted, you should take all possible steps to win over others. However, God teaches you that anyone who humbles himself will be exalted (Matthew 23:12).

Most people think that it is very natural to hate their enemy, but God tells you to "Love your enemy" and "If your enemy is hungry, feed him; if he is thirsty, give him something to drink."

God's thoughts are spiritual but men's thoughts are fleshly.

Satan gives you fleshly thoughts so that he tempts you to avoid God, disturbs you from obtaining true faith and drives you to follow worldly ways, ultimately leading to sinning and eternal death.

In Matthew 16:21 and subsequent verses, Jesus explained to His disciples that He would suffer many things, and that He should be killed on the cross and be raised to life on the third day. On hearing this, Peter took Jesus aside and began to rebuke Him, saying, *"God forbid it, Lord! This shall never happen to You"* (v. 22). However, Jesus turned and said furiously to Peter, *"Get behind Me, Satan! You are a stumbling block to Me; for you are not setting your mind on God's interests, but man's"* (v. 23). When Jesus said furiously "Get behind me, Satan," He did not mean that Peter was Satan, but that it was Satan himself that worked in Peter's thought to hinder the work of God.

That was because Jesus had to bear the cross for the salvation of mankind in accordance with the will of God, but Peter tried to prevent Him from carrying out God's will with his fleshly thoughts.

The apostle Paul writes in 2 Corinthians 10:3-6 as follows:

> *For though we walk in the flesh, we do not war according to the flesh, for the weapons of our warfare are not of the flesh, but divinely powerful for the destruction of fortresses. We are destroying speculations and every lofty thing raised up against the knowledge of God, and we are taking every thought captive to the obedience of Christ, and we are ready to punish all*

disobedience, whenever your obedience is complete.

You should demolish your own arguments and reasoning, which are set up and often work against the kingdom of God. Take captive every thought to make it obedient to Christ in order to live in accordance with truth, and then you will become a person of spirit and faith.

You should throw away the thought that you must strike someone back twice in order not to be disgraced when he strikes you because this fleshly thought is against truth.

Therefore, you should abandon all the sins coming through your thoughts. To settle the problem of sins completely, you should first of all forsake the lust of the flesh, the lust of your eyes, and the pride of life. These are the untruthful thoughts in which Satan delights.

The lusts of the flesh, that is, the thoughts arising in his mind, are desires against the will of God. Galatians 5:19-21 lists such lusts:

Now the deeds of the flesh are evident, which are: immorality, impurity, sensuality, idolatry, sorcery, enmities, strife, jealousy, outbursts of anger, disputes, dissensions, factions, envying, drunkenness, carousing, and things like these, of which I forewarn you, just as I have forewarned you, that those who practice such things will not inherit the kingdom of God.

The very desire to do what God commands you to forsake is

the lusts of the flesh.

The lust of one's eyes means that one's mind becomes heavily influenced by what he sees and hears and he starts to pursue desires that are aroused in his mind. When one loves the world seeking the lust of his eyes, only these desires seem to be valuable and he cannot be satisfied with anything.

A boastful mind arises in a person when one gets to possess the pleasure of the world in his pursuit of satisfying the cravings of a sinful man and the lust of his eyes. This is called the pride of life.

To redeem us from all kinds of immorality, lawlessness, and evil, Jesus wore a crown of thorns and shed His blood. Since only the blameless and spotless blood of Jesus could redeem us from our sins, He redeemed us from all the sins committed in our thoughts by wearing a crown of thorns on His head and shedding His blood.

Second, Jesus wore the crown of thorns to enable men to wear better crowns in heaven.

Another reason for His wearing a crown of thorns is to enable you to obtain better crowns. As He redeemed you from poverty and gave you richness by leading a poor life, so He wore the crown of thorns to enable you to obtain better crowns in heaven.

There are countless crowns prepared for the children of God in heaven. There are prizes such as gold medals, silver medals, or bronze medals given to winners according to their ranking in an athletic event. Likewise, there are various crowns in heaven.

There is an imperishable crown as described in 1 Corinthians 9:25: *"Everyone who competes in the games exercises self-control in all things. They then do it to receive a perishable wreath, but we an imperishable."* An imperishable crown is prepared for God's children who strive to cast away their sins. The crown of glory is prepared for those who cast away their sins and live in accordance with the Word of God and glorify Him (1 Peter 5:4). The crown of life is also prepared for those who greatly love God, are faithful to Him to the point of death, and become holy by forsaking every kind of evil (James 1:12; Revelation 2:10).

The crown of righteousness is given to those who, like the apostle Paul, become holy by discarding all their sins and furthermore, accomplish their mission completely in accordance with God's will (2 Timothy 4:8).

It is also described in Revelation 4:4 that *"Around the throne were twenty-four thrones; and upon the thrones I saw twenty-four elders sitting, clothed in white garments, and golden crowns on their heads."* The crown of gold is prepared for people who reach the level of an elder and who will assist God in New Jerusalem.

Here, "elders" do not refer to people who are given that title in churches of this world, but describe people recognized by God as elders because they are holy and faithful in all God's house, and have an unchangeable faith of gold.

God gives different crowns to His children depending on the extent to which they discard sins and accomplish God's mission.

The children of God will be great in heaven and will receive better crowns if they do not think about how to gratify the desires of the sinful nature and behave appropriately according to the Word of God (Romans 13:13-14), if their soul goes well with them as they live by the Spirit (Galatians 5:16), and if they faithfully perform their duty and mission!

Likewise, Jesus redeemed you from all the sins committed through your thoughts by wearing a crown of thorns and shedding blood. How thankful you should be because He prepares better crowns in heaven to give you in accordance with the measure of your faith and the fulfillment of your mission!

Therefore, you must realize how glorious it is to be qualified to receive these crowns. Then you should have the heart of your Lord by forsaking every kind of evil, do well with your mission, and be faithful in all God's house. I hope you will receive the best crown you can in heaven.

Jesus' Garments and Tunic

Jesus, who was wearing a crown of thorns and was shedding blood all over His body because of a severe whipping, came to Golgotha, a place of crucifixion. When Roman soldiers crucified Jesus, they took His clothes, dividing them into four shares, one for each of them. They did not divide the tunic but cast lots for it.

Then the soldiers, when they had crucified Jesus, took
His outer garments and made four parts, a part to every

soldier and also the tunic; now the tunic was seamless, woven in one piece. So they said to one another, "Let us not tear it, but cast lots for it, to decide whose it shall be"; this was to fulfill the Scripture: "They divided My outer garments among them, and for My clothing they cast lots" (John 19:23-24).

Why does the Word of God explain in detail about Jesus' clothes and tunic? The history of Israel since 70 A.D. is deeply embedded in the spiritual implication of this incident.

Being Stripped and Crucified

According to Matthew 27:22-26, at the request of the Israelites who did not recognize Jesus as the Messiah, Jesus was sentenced to crucifixion by Pontius Pilate after He had been mocked and despised in various ways.

After wearing a crown of thorns and being mocked and scorned, He bore the cross to Golgotha and was crucified there. Pilate ordered the soldiers to place the written charge against Him above His head, which read, *"THIS IS JESUS THE KING OF THE JEWS"* (Matthew 27:37).

The notice was written in Hebrew, Latin and Greek. Hebrew was the traditional language of the Jews, God's chosen people. Latin was the official language of the Roman Empire, the most powerful nation at that time, and Greek was the language dominating the culture of the world. Thus, the notice written in these three languages symbolizes that the whole world recognized Jesus as indeed the king of the Jews and as the King of kings.

After reading the notice, in John 19:21-22, many Jews protested to Pilate not to write, "The King of the Jews" but instead to write, "He said, 'I am King of the Jews.'" However, Pilate answered them, "What I have written, I have written," and left it unchanged. This means that even Pilate recognized Jesus as the king of the Jews.

As Pilate recognized Jesus as the king of the Jews, He is indeed the only Son of God, the King of kings, and the Lord of lords. Nevertheless, in front of many people watching Him, Jesus was stripped of His clothes and tunic and was crucified on the cross. In that way, He endured such a heartbreaking shame.

We are living in this wicked world, forgetting the whole duty of man. And to redeem us from all kinds of shame, dirty things, wickedness, lawlessness, and immorality, Jesus the King of kings was stripped His clothes and tunic and suffered shame while many people were watching Him. If you understand the spiritual meaning in this, you cannot help but be thankful for it.

Dividing Jesus' Garments into Four Shares

Roman soldiers stripped Jesus bare and crucified Him. They took His clothes and divided them into four shares but they cast lots for His tunic.

Common sense dictates that His clothes could not have been beautiful or expensive. Then why did the soldiers divide His clothes into four parts?

Did they know, in far-seeing wisdom, that Jesus would be honored as the Messiah and did they want to get even an article of clothing to give their descendants as a precious family treasure? No, that was not the case.

Psalm 22:18 prophesies, *"They divide my garments among them, and for my clothing they cast lots."* God allowed Roman soldiers to take His clothes to fulfill this verse (John 19:24).

Then, what spiritual implications do Jesus' clothes hold? Why did they divide His clothes into four shares, one for each of them? Why did they not divide his tunic? Why did God allow this story to be written in advance?

Since Jesus is the king of the Jews, Jesus' clothes refer to the nation of Israel or the Jewish people. As Roman soldiers divided the clothes into four shares, the clothes lost their shape. This implies that Israel as a nation will be destroyed. It also indicates that the name Israel will remain as the shares of the clothes remained. After all, the words written about His clothes prophesied that the Jewish people would be scattered in all directions as a result of the destruction of their nation. The history of Israel testifies that this prophecy has been fulfilled.

Within forty years of the death of Jesus on the cross, a Roman general named Titus destroyed Jerusalem. The Temple of God was destroyed completely without a stone remaining upon a stone. Since the nation of Israel ceased to exist, the Jews were scattered everywhere, persecuted, and even slaughtered.

This explains why the Jews have been living all over the world even to this day.

Matthew 27:23 depicts a gruesome scene in which Pilate tells the wicked crowd that Jesus was guiltless, but they shouted all the louder to crucify Jesus. At this, Pilate took water and washed his hands to show that he was not responsible for the death of the innocent Jesus, saying, *"I am innocent of this Man's blood; see to that yourselves."* (v. 24) Then, the crowd answered, *"His blood shall be on us and on our children!"* (v. 25)

A remarkable element is that the history of Israel clearly shows that many of the Jews and their descendants shed blood, as if to fulfill their demands to Pontius Pilate. Within four decades of Jesus' death, as many as 1.1 million Jews were slaughtered. Furthermore, during World War II, the Nazi Germany killed about six million Jewish people. The film "The Schindler's List" portrays tragic scenes in which Jewish people, with no distinction of male and female, the old and the young, were killed without wearing any clothes. Even a criminal is allowed to put on clean clothes when he is executed, but Jewish people were stripped bare when they were slaughtered.

The Jewish people had not recognized Jesus the Messiah and had stripped Him bare and crucified Him. As they shouted, "His blood shall be on us and on our children," awful distress came upon the people of Israel for ages.

Jesus' Seamless Tunic Woven in One Piece

John 19:23 describes Jesus' tunic: *"Now the tunic was seamless, woven in one piece."* Here, "seamless" in the verse means that the tunic was not stitched to join several pieces of cloth. Most people take no interest in how their clothes are made or whether their clothes are woven from top to bottom or from bottom to top. Then why does the Bible describe Jesus' tunic in detail?

The Bible tells that the forefather of all human beings is Adam, the forefather of faith is Abraham, and the forefather of Israel is Jacob. God teaches us that the forefather of Israel is not Abraham but Jacob because the twelve tribes of Israel came from Jacob's twelve sons. The founder of the nation Israel is Jacob even though the forefather of faith is Abraham.

God also blessed Jacob in Genesis 35:10-11 in this way:

> *"Your name is Jacob; You shall no longer be called Jacob, but Israel shall be your name." Thus He called him Israel. God also said to him, "I am God Almighty; be fruitful and multiply; a nation and a company of nations shall come from you, and kings shall come forth from you."*

According to the Word of God mentioned in those verses, Jacob's twelve sons formed the backbone of Israel and Israel was a united country until it was divided in the days of King Rehoboam into Israel in the North and Judah in the South.

Later, Israel in the North became mixed with Gentiles but Judah remained united. Today the people of Judah are called the Jews. The fact that the tunic of Jesus was seamless, woven from top to bottom in one piece, means that the nation Israel kept its unity and identity as descendants of Jacob to this day.

Casting Lots for Jesus' Tunic Without Tearing

Here, the tunic signifies the heart of people. Since Jesus is the king of Israel, His tunic implies the heart of the Jewish people.

The Israelites, as God's people chosen through their forefather of faith Abraham, have worshipped the true God above all things. The fact that they did not divide the tunic implies that the spirit of the Jewish people of Israel who worship God has been well preserved without being torn to pieces even though the nation or government of Israel itself was at times destroyed.

In fact, the Bible prophesied that the Gentiles could not exterminate the spirit of Israelites abiding deep in their hearts. In other words, their hearts toward God have been steadfastly maintained, even if the nation of Israel was destroyed by the Gentiles. Since they have such an unchangeable heart, God chose the Israelites as His own people and has used them to establish His kingdom and righteousness.

Even today, Israelites try to obey the Law with an unchanging heart. This is because they are the descendants of Jacob who himself had an unchangeable heart. The Israelites surprised the whole world by gaining their independence on May 14, 1948, a long time after they had lost their country. After that, they have developed rapidly as one of the advanced and influential countries, and they have displayed their national spirit and excellence once again.

As Roman soldiers could not divide Jesus' undergarment, which was seamless, woven in one piece from top to bottom, the Gentiles cannot destroy the spirit of Israelites worshipping God. After all, the Israelites as the descendants of Jacob established an independent country and fulfilled the will of God as His chosen people.

Israel at the End of Time Foretold in the Bible

As God foretold the history of Israel through Jesus' clothes and undergarment, He also gave us a hint on the last days of the world.

Ezekiel 38:8-9 reads:

After many days you will be summoned; in the latter years you will come into the land that is restored from the sword, whose inhabitants have been gathered from many nations to the mountains of Israel which had been a continual waste; but its people were brought out from the nations, and they are living securely, all of them. "You will go up, you will come like a storm; you will be like a cloud covering the land, you and all your troops, and many peoples with you."

"After many days" in the verses is the period of time from the birth of Jesus to His Second Coming, and "in the latter years" refer to the last years approaching Jesus' Second Coming. "The mountains of Israel" indicates Jerusalem, which is located on the highlands about 760 meters above sea level. Therefore, the word that in future years many people will gather from many countries predicts that the Israelites would come back to their land from all over the world when Jesus' Return draws near.

This prediction came true when Israel was destroyed by the Roman Empire in 70 A.D., and gained their independence in 1948. Israel had been desolate until it became independent, but it grew to be one of the most developed countries in the world.

The New Testament also prophesies the independence of Israel. Jesus in Matthew 24:32-34 tells us the following:

> *Now learn the parable from the fig tree: when its branch has already become tender and puts forth its leaves, you know that summer is near; So, you too, when you see all these things, recognize that He is near, right at the door. Truly I say to you, this generation will not pass away until all these things take place.*

This was Jesus' response to His disciples who had asked Him for the sign of His Second Coming and of the end of the age.

The fig tree in the verses refers to Israel. When the leaves of trees fall and the cold wind blows, you know that winter is near. Likewise, as soon as the twigs of fig tree get tender and its leaves spring out, you know that summer is near. With this parable, Jesus explains that when Israel is restored after a long time of destruction, that is, when the people of Israel gain their independence, Jesus' Second Coming will be very near.

You do not know how long "this generation" which Jesus mentioned in the verse is, but you do know that what He said would surely be fulfilled. You already witnessed the independence of Israel, so it is very easy to figure out that Jesus' Second Coming is very near.

Signs of the End of the Age

In Matthew 24, when His disciples asked for the signs of the end of the age, Jesus explained them in detail. However, He did not tell the exact hour and day, saying, *"No one knows about that day or hour, not even the angels in heaven, nor the Son, but only the Father"* (Matthew 24:36).

This only means that He as the Son of Man who came in flesh to this world did not know the exact hour or day. This does not mean that Jesus as one of the Trinity did not know it after His crucifixion, resurrection, and ascension to heaven.

Saying many things about the signs of the end of the age, Jesus warned you, *"Because lawlessness is increased, most people's love will grow cold. But the one who endures to the end, he will be saved"* (Matthew 24:12-13).

Today, you can feel keenly that wickedness is increasing and love is growing colder. You can hardly find warm-heartedness. Jesus said in Matthew 24:14, *"This gospel of the kingdom will be preached in the whole world as a testimony to all nations, and then the end will come."* The gospel has already been preached to all the corners of the earth.

Furthermore, we live in a "global village" in which every corner of the globe is accessible either via transportation or communication. This phenomenon, too, has been foretold in Daniel 12:4: *"But as for you, Daniel, conceal these words and seal up the book until the end of time; many will go back and forth, and knowledge will increase."* The gospel has been spread rapidly all throughout the world in this environment.

It is true that even if the gospel has been preached to the entire world, there may be some people who do not accept Jesus because they do not open their hearts. Or, there may be some remote places the seed of the gospel has not yet been scattered.

The prophecies in the Old Testament have all been fulfilled and most prophecies in the New Testament have almost been fulfilled as well. The whole Scripture is inspired through the Holy Spirit. Thus, the Word of God is correct and contains no error. The smallest letter or the least stroke of a pen will not be changed in the Word. God has been fulfilling His Word and promises, and only a few things remain unfulfilled, including the Second Coming of our Lord Jesus Christ, Seven Years of Great Tribulation, the Millennium, and the Great Judgment of the White Throne.

Nailed through His Hands and Feet

The crucifixion was one of the cruelest methods of execution for murderers or traitors. One's arms were stretched out on a wooden cross. The person was nailed through both hands and feet. He was hung on the cross for a long time until he died. Thus, he was to suffer from tremendous pain to the last breath.

Jesus the Son of God did only good things and had no blemish or spot in this world. Then, why was Jesus nailed through both hands and feet shedding His blood on the cross?

Pain of Being Nailed through Hands and Feet

Jesus was sentenced to death on a cross and came to the place of execution, Golgotha. One Roman soldier holding a big iron nail and the other one holding a hammer began to nail His hands and feet at the command of a centurion. Then they erected the cross. Can you imagine how painful must this have been?

The innocent Jesus had to suffer from pain when the big nails were hammered into His body and when His body was pulled down by His weight and the nailed body parts were ripped.

When one was beheaded, the pain ended in an instant. However, dying on the cross was so much more painful because one was hung, bled, and suffered from dehydration and exhaustion until the moment of His death.

Furthermore, on a sunny day in the desert, all kinds of insects and vermin flew all over His torn body to suck the blood flowing from His wounds at nailed hands and feet. On top of this, wicked people pointed their fingers at Him, spat on Him, mocked Him, cursed Him, and heaped insults upon Him. Some people even despised Him, saying, *"You who are going to destroy the temple and rebuild it in three days, save Yourself! If You are the Son of God, come down from the cross!"* (Matthew 27:40).

Unbearable pain accompanied Jesus during His crucifixion. However, Jesus knew very well that His bearing sins and curses by dying on the cross opened the way for redeeming mankind from their sins and making them children of God. His real pain instead came from another source. Still there were some people who did not know this providence of God or who did not receive salvation in their wickedness. This brought Him a greater pain.

Sins Committed With Hands and Feet

Once a sinful thought is conceived in the heart, the heart urges the hands and feet to commit sins. Since there is a spiritual law that the wages of sin is death, when you commit sins, you have to fall into Hell and suffer there forever.

That is why Jesus says, *"If your foot causes you to stumble, cut it off; it is better for you to enter life lame, than, having your two feet, to be cast into hell, [where their worm does not die, and the fire is not quenched.] If your eye causes you to stumble, throw it out; it is better for you to enter the kingdom of God with one eye, than, having two eyes, to be cast into hell"* (Mark 9:45-47).

How many times have you committed sins with your hands and feet since birth? Some beat other people in anger. Some steal and still some others lose their fortunes through gambling.

People become violent with feet and they go where they should not go. Therefore, if your feet cause you to sin, it is better to cut them off and enter heaven than to be thrown into Hell with two feet.

Also, how many sins have you committed with your eyes? Greed and adultery consume you when you see something that you should not see with your eyes. That is why Jesus said that if your eyes caused you to sin, it would be better to gouge them out and enter heaven than be thrown into Hell after committing sin with them.

During Old Testament times, if one committed sin with his eye, it was plucked out; if one committed sin with his hand or foot, his hand or foot was cut off; if one committed murder or adultery, he should be stoned to death (Deuteronomy 19:19-21).

Without the suffering of Jesus Christ on the cross, even today, the children of God should cut off their hands or feet if they commit sins with their hands or feet. However, Jesus took the cross, was nailed through His hands and feet and shed His blood. By doing this He washed away the sins committed with your hands and feet and you need not suffer any more or pay a price for your own sins. How great His love is!

You should keep in mind that He purifies you from all sins if you walk in the light as He is in the light, and if you confess your sins and turn to Him (1 John 1:7).

Therefore, it is very important that you fill your heart with the truth in order to lead a victorious life with a thankful and gracious heart that is always focused on God.

Jesus' Legs Not Broken
but His Side Pierced

The day Jesus died was a Friday, the day before the Sabbath. In those days, Saturday was observed as the Sabbath, and the Jews did not want the bodies left on crosses during the Sabbath.

Thus, as you can read in John 19:31, the Jews asked Pontius Pilate to have the legs broken and the bodies taken down.

With Pontius Pilate's permission, the soldiers broke the legs of the robbers who had been crucified on either side of Jesus but they did not break Jesus' legs because He was already dead. In those days, those who were crucified were deemed cursed and that was why the soldiers broke their legs. Therefore, there is a divine providence in the fact that they did not break Jesus' legs.

Why Were Jesus' Legs Not Broken?

Jesus, who had no sin, was cursed and hung on the cross to redeem human beings from the curse of the Law. Satan could not break His legs not because Jesus died due to His sin but by the providence of God.

Besides, God protected Jesus from having His bones broken to fulfill the words of Psalm 34:20, which reads, *"He keeps all his bones, not one of them is broken."*

In Numbers 9:12, God tells the Israelites not to break any bones of the lamb when they eat it. He also says in Exodus 12:46 that the Israelites could eat the meat of the lamb but they should not break any of its bones.

The "lamb" refers to Jesus who was spotless and blameless, yet sacrificed Himself as an atoning sacrifice for human beings and their sins out of His love for us. In accordance with Scripture Exodus 12:46, saying, *"[The lamb] is to be eaten in a single house; you are not to bring forth any of the flesh outside of the house, nor are you to break any bone of it,"* none of Jesus' bones was broken.

His Side Pierced With a Spear

John 19:32-34 depicts yet another ghastly scene:

So the soldiers came, and broke the legs of the first man and of the other who was crucified with Him; but coming to Jesus, when they saw that He was already dead, they did not break His legs. But one of the soldiers pierced His side with a spear, and immediately blood and water came out.

Even though the soldier had already known that Jesus was dead, why did he still pierce Jesus' side with a spear, bringing a sudden flow of blood and water? This illustrates the wickedness of man.

Though He was God, Jesus did not demand or cling to His rights as God. Instead, He made Himself nothing; He took the humble position of a slave and appeared in the form of a human being. He obediently humbled Himself even further by dying a criminal's death on a cross. In this manner, Jesus opened the door of salvation for you (Philippians 2:6-8).

During His life in this world, Jesus gave the prisoners freedom, gave the poor richness, and healed the sick and the weak. He did not have enough time to eat or sleep as He did His best to proclaim the Word of God to save as many souls as He could. He went to a hill to pray even when His disciples were resting.

Many Jews persecuted Him with disdain although He did only good. In the end, they crucified Him on a cross out of their wickedness. Furthermore, in spite of knowing He was dead, a Roman soldier pierced Him with a spear. This tells us that people were heaping wickedness upon wickedness.

God showed you His tremendous love by sending His only Son Jesus Christ and having Him be crucified on a cross to redeem you from sins, regardless of the wickedness of human beings.

Shedding the Blood and Water from His Side

As already mentioned, a Roman soldier pierced Jesus' side with a spear in his wickedness, regardless of his knowledge of Jesus' death. When the soldier pierced His side, blood and water flowed from the body of Jesus. There are three meanings in this episode.

First, it shows you that Jesus came in flesh as the Son of Man. John 1:14 says, *"And the Word became flesh, and dwelt among us, and we saw His glory, glory as of the only begotten from the Father, full of grace and truth."* God came to this world in flesh and He was Jesus.

Sinners cannot see God because they perish upon seeing Him. Thus, God cannot appear directly before them and that is why Jesus came to this world in flesh and showed many proofs to lead us to believe in God.

The Bible tells you that Jesus was a man just like you. Mark 3:20 reads, *"And He came home, and the crowd gathered again, to such an extent that they could not even eat a meal."* Matthew 8:24 tells us, *"And behold, there arose a great storm on the sea, so that the boat was being covered with the waves; but Jesus Himself was asleep."*

Some people may wonder how Jesus the Son of God could be hungry or in pain. However, since Jesus was in flesh composed of bones and muscles, He had to eat and sleep. He also suffered from pain the way we do.

The fact that blood and water flowed from His body when He was pierced with a spear, gives you a convincing proof that Jesus came to this world in flesh, although He is the Son of God.

Second, it is another proof that you can also participate in the divine nature even if you have flesh. God wants His children to be holy and perfect as He is. So He says, *"You shall be holy, for I am holy"* (1 Peter 1:16) and *"Therefore you are to be perfect, as your heavenly Father is perfect"* (Matthew 5:48). He also encourages you by saying, *"For by these He has granted to us His precious and magnificent promises, so that by them you may become partakers of the divine nature, having escaped the corruption that is in the world by lust"* (2 Peter 1:4), and *"Have this attitude in yourselves which was also in Christ Jesus"* (Philippians 2:5).

Jesus came to this world in flesh and became a servant according to the will of God, and fulfilled His whole duty. He also fulfilled the Law with love by overcoming all the trials and troubles, and living according to the Word of God.

Although He was a man just like you, He willingly accepted all the pain, followed God's will with endurance and self-control, and sacrificed Himself in love to die on a cross without resistance or complaints.

How, then, can we participate in the divine nature with the heart of Christ Jesus?

You must crucify your sinful nature, consisting of passion and desire, have spiritual love and pray earnestly to participate in the divine nature by having the same attitude as that of Jesus.

On the one hand, fleshly love is self-seeking, and this love becomes cold as time goes by. People with this kind of love betray each other and suffer from pain when they are not in one accord.

On the other hand, God wants you to have the love that is patient, kind and not self-centered. Thus, it is the spiritual love that never changes and flourishes day by day. You can have the attitude of Jesus as much as you possess the spiritual love and as much as you throw away every kind of evil through earnest prayer.

Likewise, everyone can receive God's grace and power if he seeks His help in fasting and earnest prayer. God also works for him to get rid of every kind of evil. You will shine like the sun in the heavenly kingdom if you possess spiritual love, produce the nine fruit of the Holy Spirit (Galatians 5) and receive the Beatitudes (Matthew 5).

Third, Jesus' shed blood and water is powerful enough to lead you to a true and eternal life.

The blood and water of Jesus was spotless and blameless since He had no original sin and committed no sin. Spiritually, it was this blood and water that could be resurrected. Because He shed His holy blood, your sins are purified and you can possess true life leading to salvation, resurrection, and eternal life.

The water, which flowed from the body of Jesus, symbolizes the everlasting water, the Word of God. You can be filled with truth and be a true child of God to the extent you understand His Word and throw away your sins by living according to it.

Jesus, without any spot or blemish, gave up all things to give you a true life to the point of shedding blood and water, even though you were no better than animals.

I hope you understand that you are saved without having paid any price and throw away sins by praying earnestly in faith so that you can lead a fruitful life in Jesus Christ.

Chapter 7

THE LAST SEVEN WORDS OF JESUS ON THE CROSS

- Father, Forgive Them
- Today You Shall Be With Me in Paradise
- Dear Woman, Here Is Your Son;
  Here Is Your Mother
- *Eloi, Eloi, Lama Sabachthani?*
- I Am Thirsty
- It Is Finished
- Father, Into Your Hands
  I Commit My Spirit

But Jesus was saying, "Father, forgive them; for they do not know what they are doing." And they cast lots, dividing up His garments among themselves.

And he was saying, "Jesus, remember me when You come in Your kingdom!" And He said to him, "Truly I say to you, today you shall be with Me in Paradise." It was now about the sixth hour, and darkness fell over the whole land until the ninth hour, because the sun was obscured; and the veil of the temple was torn in two. And Jesus, crying out with a loud voice, said, "Father, into Your hands I commit My spirit." Having said this, He breathed His last.

Luke 23:34, 42-46

Most people recall their lives when death comes near. To their family members and friends they leave last words.

In the same way, Jesus became flesh, came to this world in God's providence, and proclaimed the seven words on the cross as He breathed His last. These are called "The Last Seven Words of Jesus on the Cross."

Let us examine the spiritual meanings of Jesus' last seven words on the cross.

Father, Forgive Them

The author of Philippians describes Jesus in the following way. Jesus:

> Have this attitude in yourselves which was also in Christ Jesus, who, although He existed in the form of God, did not regard equality with God a thing to be grasped, but emptied Himself, taking the form of a bond-servant, and being made in the likeness of men. Being found in appearance as a man, He humbled Himself by becoming obedient to the point of death, even death on a cross (Philippians 2:5-8).

Jesus was crucified on the cross to demonstrate His love and obedience to God so that He could open the way of salvation for sinners. The people standing by the cross mocked Jesus with the leaders, *"He saved others; let Him save Himself if this is the Christ of God, His Chosen One"* (Luke 23:35).

The soldiers also mocked Him, offering Him sour wine, and said, *"If You are the King of the Jews, save Yourself!"* (v. 37) One of the criminals who were hanged there was hurling abuse at Him, saying, *"Are You not the Christ? Save Yourself and us!"* (v. 39)

> *When they came to the place called The Skull, there they crucified Him and the criminals, one on the right and the other on the left. But Jesus was saying, "Father, forgive them; for they do not know what they are doing." And they cast lots, dividing up His garments among themselves* (Luke 23:33-34).

Jesus prayed to God asking for their forgiveness, "Father, forgive them; for they do not know what they are doing," while He breathed His last. Jesus petitioned the Father to give mercy and forgiveness to people who did not know that Jesus the Son of God was being crucified to forgive their sins. Perhaps they did not even realize their actions were sin. This is His first word from the cross.

Jesus Prays in Love for People Crucifying Him

Jesus, the Son of God, prayed for those who crucified Him even though He had neither defect nor blemish. How deep and great His love is! Jesus could have easily come down from the cross to avoid His crucifixion since He is one with God the Almighty and is empowered by God the Father. However, He was crucified to fulfill the plan of salvation according to God's will. Therefore, He could endure all the sufferings and shame, pray for them in desperate love and ask for their forgiveness.

Jesus prayed earnestly, "Father, forgive them; for they do not know what they are doing." Here, "they" does not simply refer to those who crucified and mocked Him, but also include all human beings who do not receive Jesus Christ and continue to live in the darkness. Like the people who crucified Jesus the Son of God, many people are sinning because they do not know Jesus Christ and the truth.

Your enemy the devil belongs to the darkness and hates the light so he crucified Jesus, the true light. Today, the devil controls people who belong to the darkness and causes them to persecute those who walk in the light.

How can you react to persecutors who do not know truth?

Jesus teaches you what God's will is and what a Christian's attitude should be through the first word from the cross. In Matthew 5:44, it says, *"But I say to you, love your enemies and pray for those who persecute you."* So we must be able to pray for all those who persecute us, saying, "Father, forgive them. They do not know what they are doing. Bless them so that they,

146 _ THE MESSAGE OF THE CROSS

too, may receive the Lord and we can meet again in heaven."

Today You Shall Be With Me in Paradise

Two criminals were also crucified when Jesus was hung on the cross that stood high on Golgotha, "the place of the Skull" (Luke 23:33).

One of the criminals hurled insults at Him but the other rebuked the first criminal, repented, and accepted Jesus as his personal Savior. Then Jesus promised him that He would be in Paradise with him. That is the second word of Jesus on the cross.

> One of the criminals who were hanged there was hurling abuse at Him, saying, "Are You not the Christ? Save Yourself and us!" But the other answered, and rebuking him said, "Do you not even fear God, since you are under the same sentence of condemnation? And we indeed are suffering justly, for we are receiving what we deserve for our deeds; but this man has done nothing wrong." And he was saying, "Jesus, remember me when You come in Your kingdom!" And He said to him, "Truly I say to you, today you shall be with Me in Paradise" (Luke 23:39-43).

Jesus proclaimed He was the Messiah who could forgive sinners when they repented and save them through His second word from the cross.

When you read the Four Gospels, the two criminals' responses are written in different ways. In Matthew 27:44, it says, *"The robbers who had been crucified with Him were also insulting Him with the same words."* In Mark 15:32, it reads, *"'Let this Christ, the King of Israel, now come down from the cross, so that we may see and believe!' Those who were crucified with Him were also insulting Him."* From these two Gospels, you read that both criminals heaped insults on Jesus.

However, in Luke 23, you read that one criminal rebuked the other and repented of his sins, accepted Jesus Christ and was saved. This was not because the Gospels are not in accordance with each other. Instead, in His providence, God allowed the authors to write in different ways. In the Bible God's providence and historical elements are condensed. If everything were written in detail, a thousand Bibles would not suffice.

Today, if you record something with a video camera, you can watch it later but in Jesus' time, there was no such equipment so they could not take even one photograph even though these were very important incidents. They could only write these events. Through slight differences, you can experience and relive a particular situation more realistically.

The Better Understanding of Jesus' Crucifixion

When Jesus proclaimed the gospel, large crowds followed Him. Some wanted to listen to His message, some wanted to see miracles and signs from heaven, others wanted food, and still others sold their properties to serve and follow Jesus.

In Luke 9, Jesus gave thanks for five loaves of bread and two fish. The number of those who ate was about five thousand men (Luke 9:12-17). Imagine how many more people, including those who loved or hated Jesus and others in the crowd must have gathered in the place where He was crucified. The crowd surrounded the cross so the soldiers blocked them with spears and shields. Imagine the people yelling at Jesus in a circle near the cross. The crowd was insulting Him. Even one of the two criminals hanging on either side of Jesus insulted Him.

Who would have been able to hear what the first criminal said? It was more than likely very rowdy so only the people standing close enough to Jesus could hear His words. The other criminal said something towards Jesus with a bad facial expression. This criminal, in fact, was rebuking that criminal who had insulted Jesus. However, those who were far in the opposite side might have easily thought that this repenting criminal was rebuking Jesus in the middle.

On the one hand, in that noisy condition, each writer of the Gospels of Matthew and Mark who could not hear the repenting criminal clearly thought that he also rebuked Jesus. So they wrote that both criminals rebuked Jesus.

On the other hand, the writer of the Gospel of Luke heard clearly, so he knew one of the two criminals did not insult but instead repented. Different writers were in different locations and wrote differently.

God, who knows everything, allowed them to write in different ways so that later generations could discern a particular situation clearly.

Heavenly Place for the Repented Criminal

Jesus promised the criminal who repented on the cross before death, "You shall be with Me in Paradise." It has a spiritual meaning.

Heaven, God's kingdom, is very vast beyond your imagination. Even Jesus told us in John 14:2, *"In My Father's house are many dwelling places; if it were not so, I would have told you; for I go to prepare a place for you."* The psalmist urges us to *"Praise Him, highest heavens, and the waters that are above the heavens!"* (Psalm 148:4) Nehemiah 9:6 praises God who made the heavens, even the highest heavens. 2 Corinthians 12:2 speaks of *"a man in Christ who fourteen years ago whether in the body I do not know, or out of the body I do not know, God knows such a man was caught up to the third heaven."* In Revelation 21:2, it says that in New Jerusalem dwells God's throne.

Likewise, there are many dwelling places in heaven. However, you are not allowed to live in any place of your choosing. The God of justice rewards each of you according to what you have done in this world: how much you imitate your Lord and work for the kingdom of God and how much you store up in heaven, etc (Matthew 11:12; Revelation 22:12).

John 3:6 reads, *"That which is born of the flesh is flesh, and that which is born of the Spirit is spirit."* Depending on the extent one rids himself of fleshly things and becomes a spiritual person, dwelling places in heaven will be divided into groups of the same spiritual level.

Of course, every place in heaven is very beautiful because God reigns it. However, there are differences even within heaven. For instance, lifestyle, hobbies, living standards, and the like in a metropolis are vastly different from those in countryside. In the same manner, the holy city, New Jerusalem, is the most glorious place in heaven where God's throne is housed and where the children who resemble Him the most will reside.

However, Paradise is the place where the repentant criminal in the last minute of his death on the cross lives and is located on the outskirts of heaven. Many others who receive shameful salvation will live there. These people received Jesus Christ but did not step forward to be changed spiritually.

Why did the repentant criminal enter Paradise?

He confessed that he was a sinner in his good heart, and received Jesus as his Savior. However, he did not get rid of his sins, live according to the Word of God, or evangelize others. He did not work for the Lord. He did not do anything to receive any heavenly prize. That is why he entered Paradise, the lowliest place in heaven.

Jesus' Descent to the Upper Grave

Even though Jesus promised the criminal, "Today you shall be with Me in Paradise," it does not mean Jesus lives only in Paradise in heaven. Jesus, the King of kings and the Lord of lords, governs and dwells with God's children in all of heaven, including Paradise and New Jerusalem. In this sense He dwells in Paradise as well as other places within heaven.

When Jesus told the saved criminal "Today you shall be with Me in Paradise," "today" does not simply refer to the specific day Jesus died on the cross or any other particular day. Jesus mentioned that He would be with the repentant criminal wherever the criminal was from the moment he became God's child.

When you refer to the Bible, Jesus did not go to Paradise after His death. In Matthew 12:40, Jesus tells some of the Pharisees that *"Just as Jonah was three days and three nights in the belly of the sea monster, so will the Son of Man be three days and three nights in the heart of the earth."* Ephesians 4:9 reads, *"Now this expression, 'He ascended,' what does it mean except that He also had descended into the lower parts of the earth?"*

In addition, 1 Peter 3:18-19 says, *"For Christ also died for sins once for all, the just for the unjust, so that He might bring us to God, having been put to death in the flesh, but made alive in the spirit; in which also He went and made proclamation to the spirits now in prison."* Jesus went to the Upper Grave and preached the gospel to the spirits before He was resurrected on the third day. Why was this necessary?

Before Jesus came to this world, many people during Old Testament times and people even in New Testament times did not have a chance to hear the gospel but they lived in goodness accepting God. Does this mean they all went to Hell just because they did not know who Jesus is?

God sent His only Son to this world and whoever receives Him will be saved. God would not have started human cultivation to save only those who receive Jesus Christ after His crucifixion. Those who did not have a chance to hear the gospel but lived with good conscience will be judged according to their conscience.

On the one hand, those people good in heart gather like this in the "Upper Grave." On the other hand, the "Lower Grave," which is also referred to as "Hades," is where the wicked souls are to live until the Judgment Day. After His crucifixion, Jesus went to the Upper Grave and preached the gospel to the spirits who did not know the gospel but lived with good conscience and were worthy to be saved.

There is no other name under heaven given to men by which they must be saved but Jesus Christ. That is why Jesus went and preached about Himself to the spirits so that they could receive Him and be saved.

The Bible says that the spirits saved before Jesus' crucifixion are carried to Abraham's side (Luke 16:22), but are carried to Jesus' side after His resurrection.

Salvation According to the Judgment of Conscience

Before Jesus came to this world to spread the gospel, good people had lived by following the righteousness in their hearts. That is the law of conscience. Good people did not do evil even when they had troubles and faced difficulties, because they listened to the voice of their hearts.

Romans 1:20 reads, *"For since the creation of the world His invisible attributes, His eternal power and divine nature, have been clearly seen, being understood through what has been made, so that they are without excuse."*

By seeing the universe and how everything on earth is in harmony, people with good hearts believe that there is eternal life. This is why they do not live according to their sinful nature and they control themselves not to enjoy worldly pleasures in fear of God.

Romans 2:14-15 reads, *"For when Gentiles who do not have the Law do instinctively the things of the Law, these, not having the Law, are a law to themselves, in that they show the work of the Law written in their hearts, their conscience bearing witness and their thoughts alternately accusing or else defending them."*

God gave the Law only to the Israelites but not to the Gentiles. However, it is as though the Gentiles are living by the Law when they live according to the law in their hearts, their consciences that are gained and practiced by themselves. You cannot say that those who did not believe in Jesus Christ cannot be saved because they never heard the gospel in their lives.

Among those who died without knowing Jesus Christ, there were some people who could control themselves against evil thoughts because of their clean hearts. These people will be saved according to God's judgment of their conscience.

Dear Woman, Here Is Your Son; Here Is Your Mother

The apostle John wrote what he saw and heard from the cross

on which Jesus was hanging. There were many women including Mary, Jesus' mother; Salome, His mother's sister; Mary the wife of Clopas; and Mary Magdalene. In John 19:26-27, Jesus tells the saddened Mary His mother to think of John as her son and tells John to take care of her as his mother:

> *When Jesus then saw His mother, and the disciple whom He loved standing nearby, He said to His mother, "Woman, behold, your son!" Then He said to the disciple, "Behold, your mother!" From that hour the disciple took her into his own household.*

Why Did Jesus Call Mary "Woman," Not "Mother"?

The word "mother" is not spoken by Jesus, but written by the apostle John from his perspective. Why, then, did Jesus call His own mother who had given birth to Him "woman"?

When you refer to the Bible, Jesus did not call her "mother."

For example, in John 2:1-11, Jesus performed the first miracle of turning water into wine after He started His ministry. This miracle occurred at a wedding at Cana in Galilee. Jesus and His disciples had also been invited to the wedding. When the wine ran out, Mary told Him, "They have no wine" because she knew as the Son of God, Jesus was able to change water into wine. Then Jesus told her, *"Woman, what does that have to do with us? My hour has not yet come"* (v. 4).

Jesus answered that the time for Him to show Himself as the Messiah had not yet come even though Mary felt sorry for the guests because there was no more wine left. Changing water into wine spiritually means that Jesus would shed His blood on the cross.

Jesus proclaimed about Himself that He had come to this world as our Savior by completing the divine plan for human salvation on the cross. So He called Mary "woman," not "mother."

Besides, our Savior Jesus is God in Trinity and the Creator. God the Creator is Who HE IS (Exodus 3:14), and He is the First and the Last (Revelation 1:17, 2:8). Hence, Jesus does not have a mother and that is why Jesus called her "woman," not "mother."

Today, many children of God refer to Mary as Jesus' "holy mother" or even make her statues and worship before them. You should understand that this is absolutely wrong because she is not the mother of our Savior (Exodus 20:4).

The Heavenly Citizenship

Jesus comforted Mary who was in great distress by His crucifixion and told His beloved disciple John to look after Mary as his own mother. Even though Jesus suffered from tremendous pain on the cross, He still cared deeply about what would happen to Mary after His death. You can experience His love here.

Through Jesus' third word on the cross, we can realize that in faith, we are all brothers and sisters—God's family. In Matthew 12 is a scene in which Jesus' family comes to see Him. When

Jesus is told that His mother and brothers are standing outside, He tells the crowd:

> But Jesus answered the one who was telling Him and said, "Who is My mother and who are My brothers?" And stretching out His hand toward His disciples, He said, "Behold My mother and My brothers! For whoever does the will of My Father who is in heaven, he is My brother and sister and mother" (Matthew 12:48-50).

As your faith grows after receiving Jesus Christ, your sense of citizenship in heaven becomes clearer and you love your brothers and sisters in Christ more than your biological family members. If your family members are not God's children, your family could not last as a "family" forever. Your family relationship ends with death. If they do not believe in Jesus Christ or do not live by God's will even if they claim to believe in God, they will go to Hell because the wages of sin is death (Matthew 7:21).

Your visible flesh goes back to the dust after death but you have an immortal spirit. If God takes your spirit, you will be just a corpse that will rot soon. God the Creator formed the first man from the dust and breathed the breath of life into his nostrils, so his spirit became immortal. It is God who gives birth to your immortal spirit and makes the flesh that will return to the dust. Therefore, He is your true Father.

Matthew 23:9 tells us *"Do not call anyone on earth your father; for One is your Father, He who is in heaven."* This does not mean that you should not love your non-believers in your family. It is very important that you truly love them, preach them the gospel and lead them to accept Jesus Christ.

Eloi, Eloi, Lama Sabachthani?

Jesus was crucified on the cross at the third hour, and from sixth hour, darkness came over the whole earth until the ninth hour when He breathed His last. To convert this to the modern conception of time, He was crucified at nine o'clock in the morning and three hours later, at noon, darkness came over the whole earth until three in the afternoon.

When the sixth hour came, darkness fell over the whole land until the ninth hour. At the ninth hour Jesus cried out with a loud voice, "Eloi, Eloi, lama sabachthani?" which is translated, "My God, My God, why have You forsaken Me?" (Mark 15:33-34)

Six hours later, at the ninth hour, Jesus cried out to God, "Eloi, Eloi, lama sabachthani?" It is the fourth word of Jesus from the cross.

Jesus was exhausted, for He had been hung on the cross for six hours pouring His blood and water out under the strong sun of the desert. He was thoroughly exhausted. Why, then, did He cry out?

Each of the seven words of Jesus on the cross has spiritual

meanings. If they had not been audible, they would have been useless. The seven words were intended to be written in the Bible clearly, so that everyone can understand God's will.

Therefore, He cried out the seven words from the cross with all His effort so that those around the cross could hear clearly and write them down.

Some say that Jesus shouted in resentment of God, because He had to come to this world in flesh and endure great pain needlessly. However, that is absolutely not true.

Why Did Jesus Cry Out, *"Eloi, Eloi, Lama Sabachthani?"*

The reason He came to the earth was to destroy the work of the devil and open up the door of salvation for us.

Thus, Jesus obeyed God's will to the point of death and entirely sacrificed Himself. Before His crucifixion, He prayed more earnestly and His sweat was like drops of blood falling to the ground (Luke 22:42-44). He carried His burden, fully knowing the suffering He would endure on the cross.

He endured maltreatment and suffering on the cross because He knew God's plan for human beings. How, then, could Jesus resent facing His death? His crying was not a sigh for grief or reproach to God. Jesus had reasons to do it.

First, Jesus wanted to proclaim to the world that He was being crucified to redeem all sinners from sin.
He wanted everyone to understand that He had left His

glory in Heaven and was disregarded completely by God even though He was the only begotten Son of God. He cried out to let everyone know that He was suffering from tremendous pain on the cross to save and redeem sinners from sin. The Bible shows He used to call God "my Father," but on the cross Jesus called Him, "my God." This is because Jesus took the cross on behalf of sinners and sinners cannot call God "Father."

At that moment, God had disgraced Jesus as a sinner carrying all sins of human beings, and Jesus could not dare call God "Father." In the same way you call God "Abba Father" when you have mutual love but call Him "God" instead of "Father" when you are away from God because you commit sins or have weak faith.

God wants all men to become His true children who can call Him "Father" by accepting Jesus Christ and walking in the light.

Second, Jesus wanted to warn people who did not know God's will and still lived in the darkness.

God sent His only Son Jesus Christ to this world and allowed Him to be mocked and crucified by His own creatures. Jesus knew why God disregarded His Son but the crowd who crucified Him did not know God's will. He shouted "My God, My God, why have You forsaken Me?" to let the ignorant understand God's love and repent so that they might turn back to the way of salvation.

I Am Thirsty

In the Old Testament, there are a great number of prophecies about Jesus' sufferings on the cross. In Psalm 69:21, it says, *"They also gave me gall for my food and for my thirst they gave me vinegar to drink."* As it is foretold in Psalm, when Jesus said, "I am thirsty," people soaked a sponge in wine vinegar, put the sponge on a stalk of the hyssop plant, and lifted it to Jesus' lips.

> *After this, Jesus, knowing that all things had already been accomplished, to fulfill the Scripture, said, "I am thirsty." A jar full of sour wine was standing there; so they put a sponge full of the sour wine upon a branch of hyssop and brought it up to His mouth* (John 19:28-29).

Long before Jesus Christ was born in the town of Bethlehem, the psalmist saw in a vision that Jesus would be crucified and die on the cross, and wrote on it. Jesus said, "I am thirsty" so that Scripture would be fulfilled.

Let us think about the spiritual meaning of Jesus' fifth word on the cross, "I am thirsty."

Jesus Declares His Spiritual Thirst

Many people can endure hunger but not thirst. Jesus was thoroughly exhausted because He had been nailed to the cross for six hours and shed His blood under the blazing sun of the desert. The degree of His thirst was beyond imagination.

This is not to say that Jesus could not stand His thirst when He said, "I am thirsty." He knew He would return to God in peace very soon.

In fact, He had more pain from spiritual thirst than physical thirst. That is Jesus' strong desire to God's children: "I am thirsty for I have shed My blood. Relieve My thirst by paying for My blood."

Two thousand years have passed since Jesus' death on the cross, but He is still telling us He is thirsty. His thirst was from the shedding of His blood. He shed His blood to forgive your sins and give you an eternal life.

Jesus tells you He is thirsty in order to demonstrate His willingness to save those lost souls. Therefore, God's children who are saved by Jesus' blood have to compensate for His blood.

The way you pay for His blood and quench His thirst is to lead people on their unknowing path to hell to heaven.

Therefore, you must be grateful for Jesus who shed His blood and now quench His thirst by leading people to the way of salvation.

It Is Finished

In John 19:30, Jesus received the drink and said, *"It is finished"* and bowed His head and gave up His spirit. Jesus accepted the sponge on a stalk of hyssop plant. It was not because He could not stand His thirst. There is a spiritual meaning in His deed.

The reason Jesus came in flesh to this world was to be crucified on the cross for mankind's sins. In His great love for us, Jesus fulfilled the Law of the Old Testament and bore all human beings' sins and curses on their behalf. During Old Testament times, people offered sacrifice of animals' blood to God when they sinned. However, Jesus made a single sacrifice for sins for all time by shedding His blood (Hebrews 10:11-12). Thus, your sins are forgiven when you receive Jesus Christ because He has already redeemed you. Redemptive grace through Jesus Christ refers to new wine, and He drank the wine vinegar to give us new wine.

The Spiritual Meaning of the Word "It Is Finished"

Jesus said, "It is finished" and gave up His spirit. What does this mean spiritually?

Jesus became flesh, came to the earth, preached the gospel, healed all weaknesses and diseases, and opened up the way of salvation by taking the cross for all those who had been destined to death.

He fulfilled the Law of the Old Testament with love as He sacrificed Himself to the point of death. Also, He won over the devil wholly destroying the devil's work. That is, He completed the divine plan for human salvation. That is why Jesus said, "It is finished" on the cross.

God wants His children to fulfill everything by living according to the will of God just as His only begotten Son Jesus fulfilled all providences of salvation by obeying the Father to the point of sacrificing His life according to the will and plan of God.

Thus, you must first imitate your Lord's heart by gaining spiritual love: bearing the nine fruit of the Holy Spirit (Galatians 5:22-23) and accomplishing the Beatitudes (Matthew 5:3-10). Then you have to be faithful to the work given to you by the Lord. You must lead as many people to the Lord in praying earnestly, preaching the gospel, and serving the church.

I hope that each of you, God's precious child, will overcome the world with firm faith, hope for heaven and love for God, and confess, "It is finished" by obeying God and His will the way our Lord Jesus Christ demonstrated.

Father, Into Your Hands I Commit My Spirit

By the time He uttered His last words on the cross, Jesus was utterly exhausted. In this condition, Jesus called out with a loud voice, "Father, into Your hands I commit My spirit."

> *And Jesus, crying out with a loud voice, said, "Father, into Your hands I commit My spirit." Having said this, He breathed His last* (Luke 23:46).

You may notice that Jesus called God "Father" instead of "My God." This indicates that Jesus has now completed His mission as an atoning sacrifice.

Jesus Committed His Spirit and Soul to God

Why did Jesus, who came to the earth as our Savior, commit His spirit and soul into His Father's hands?

Man is composed of spirit, soul and body (1 Thessalonians 5:23). When he dies, his spirit and soul leave his body. His spirit and soul will go back to God's side if he is a child of God. Otherwise, his spirit and soul will go to Hell (Luke 16:19-31). His body is buried and returns to the dust.

Jesus, the Son of God, became flesh and came to this world. He had spirit, soul, and body the way we do. As He was crucified, His body died but not His spirit and soul; He committed His spirit and soul into God's hands.

God receives both your spirit and soul when you die. If God receives only the spirit but not the soul, you will never experience the true happiness in heaven or be thankful from the bottom of your heart. Why? You will not remember things that come out of your soul such as tears, sorrow, suffering and other things you endured on this earth. That is why God receives both the spirit and the soul.

Why, then, did Jesus commit His spirit and soul to God? It is because God is the Creator, who governs over everything in the universe and takes care of your life, death, curse, and blessing. That is to say, everything belongs to God and is under His sovereignty. God is the only One who answers your prayers. Thus, Jesus Himself had to pray in order to commit His spirit and soul to Father God (Matthew 10:29-31).

Jesus Prayed in a Loud Voice

Why did Jesus pray in a loud voice even though He was in the midst of great suffering, saying, "Father, into Your hands I commit My spirit"?

This was because He wanted people to hear and let them know that crying out in prayer was God's will. His prayer for committing His spirit to God was as earnest as His prayer at Gethsemane shortly before His arrest.

Also, Jesus' prayer, "Father, into Your hands I commit My spirit," proves that Jesus fulfilled everything according to God's will. That is, He could now commit His spirit to God in a proud manner after He had completed His work in full obedience to God.

The apostle Paul confessed, *"I have fought the good fight, I have finished the course, I have kept the faith; in the future there is laid up for me the crown of righteousness, which the Lord, the righteous Judge, will award to me on that day; and not only to me, but also to all who have loved His appearing"* (2 Timothy 4:7-8).

Deacon Stephen also lived according to God's will and maintained the faith. That is why he could pray, *"Lord Jesus, receive my spirit"* as he drew his last breath (Acts 7:59). The apostle Paul and Stephen could not have prayed in that manner if they had led worldly lives, in pursuit of the pleasures stemming from the sinful nature.

Likewise, you can proudly say, "It is finished" and "Father, into Your hands I commit My spirit," the way Jesus did, when you have lived only according to the will of Father God.

What Happened After Jesus' Death?

Jesus died on the cross after leaving His last words in a loud voice. It was ninth hour (three o'clock in the afternoon). Even though it was daytime, darkness came over the whole land from the sixth (noon) to the ninth hour and the curtain of the temple was split in two (Luke 23:44-45).

> *And behold, the veil of the temple was torn in two from top to bottom; and the earth shook and the rocks were split. The tombs were opened, and many bodies of the saints who had fallen asleep were raised; and coming out of the tombs after His resurrection they entered the holy city and appeared to many* (Matthew 27:51-53).

There is an important spiritual meaning in the phrase, "the veil of the temple was torn in two from top to bottom." The long curtain of the temple was to divide the Holy Place from the Holy of Holies. No one could enter the Holy Place except the priest and only the high priest could enter the Holy of Holies once a year.

The tearing of the curtain of the temple indicates that Jesus offered Himself as a peace offering to tear down the wall of sins. Before the curtain was torn in two, the high priest gave sin offerings on behalf of people and mediated them to God.

You can have a direct relationship with God because the wall of sins has been torn down through Jesus' death. That is, whoever believes in Jesus Christ can enter the holy sanctuary and worship and pray to God without mediation of high priests or prophets.

Therefore, the author of Hebrews remarks, *"Therefore, brethren, since we have confidence to enter the holy place by the blood of Jesus, by a new and living way which He inaugurated for us through the veil, that is, His flesh"* (Hebrews 10:19-20).

In addition, the earth shook and the rocks split. All these unnatural events tell you the whole nature in this world was shaken. It was a representation of God's grief brought upon by man's wickedness. God expressed that He was deeply hurt because man's heart was too hardened to receive Jesus Christ even though He had given His only Son to save them.

Tombs broke open and the bodies of many holy people who had died were raised to life. It is the evidence of resurrection that whoever believes in Jesus Christ is forgiven and lives again.

Therefore, I hope you understand the spiritual meanings and the love of the Lord in His last seven words on the cross so that you can lead a victorious Christian life longing for the Lord's appearing like the forefathers of faith.

Chapter 8

TRUE FAITH AND ETERNAL LIFE

- What a Great Mystery It Is!
- False Confessions Do Not Lead to Salvation
- The Flesh and the Blood of the Son of Man
- Forgiveness Only by Walking in the Light
- Faith Accompanied with Action Is True Faith

"He who eats My flesh and drinks My blood has eternal life, and I will raise him up on the last day. For My flesh is true food, and My blood is true drink. He who eats My flesh and drinks My blood abides in Me, and I in him. As the living Father sent Me, and I live because of the Father, so he who eats Me, he also will live because of Me."

John 6:54-57

The ultimate goal of believing in Jesus Christ and attending church is to be saved and to gain eternal life. However, many people think that they would be saved just by going to church on Sundays and saying they believe in Jesus Christ, without living according to God's Word.

Of course, as it says in Galatians 2:16, *"Nevertheless knowing that a man is not justified by the works of the Law but through faith in Christ Jesus, even we have believed in Christ Jesus, so that we may be justified by faith in Christ and not by the works of the Law; since by the works of the Law no flesh will be justified,"* you cannot enter Heaven or be justified just by observing the Law outwardly, especially when your heart is full of wickedness. You have no relationship with Jesus Christ, if you keep on committing sins and do not follow God's Word even after you have learned it.

Therefore, you should realize that it is difficult for you to be saved just by professing your faith with lips. The blood of Jesus Christ purifies you from your sins to save you only when you walk in the light and live in the truth. You should have true faith accompanied by deed (1 John 1:5-7).

Now, let us consider in detail how to have true faith in order to receive whole salvation and eternal life as genuine children of God.

What a Great Mystery It Is!

It reads in Ephesians 5:31-32, *"For this reason a man shall leave his father and mother and shall be joined to his wife, and the two shall become one flesh. This mystery is great; but I am speaking with reference to Christ and the church."*

It is common sense that people leave their parents and are united with their husband or wife when they grow up. Why, then, did God say this was a great mystery? If you interpret and understand this verse literally, you would not know what this "great mystery" is, but if you realize the spiritual meaning behind it, you will be filled with joy.

The "church" here refers to children of God who have received the Holy Spirit. Namely, God compared the relationship between Jesus Christ and believers with that of between man and woman being united.

How can you leave the world and be united with your Bridegroom Jesus Christ?

If You Accept Jesus Christ by Faith

Since the first man Adam committed sin by disobeying God, sin entered this world. All his descendants became slaves of sin and children of the enemy devil who rules over this world.

You used to belong to this world and the enemy devil, who has the power of this world of darkness, before you accepted Jesus Christ. This has been confirmed by John 8:44, which reads, *"You are of your father the devil, and you want to do the desires of your father. He was a murderer from the beginning, and does not stand in the truth because there is no truth in him. Whenever he speaks a lie, he speaks from his own nature, for he is a liar and the father of lies,"* and by 1 John 3:8, *"the one who practices sin is of the devil; for the devil has sinned from the beginning."*

However, when you accept Jesus Christ as your Savior and come to the light, you receive the authority as God's child and become freed from sins, because your sins are forgiven through the blood of Jesus Christ.

If you possess the faith that Jesus Christ has redeemed you from your sins by taking His cross, God gives you the Holy Spirit as a gift, and the Holy Spirit gives birth to spirit in your heart. The Holy Spirit tells you and teaches you the will of God for you to behave and live within the truth.

You then become a child of God led by the Spirit of God, by Him you cry, "Abba Father" (Romans 8:14-15), and inherit the kingdom of heaven.

How wonderful and mysterious it is that the children of the devil who once had to fall into eternal death have become children of God who are now led to heaven through faith!

When you are united with Jesus Christ by believing in Him, the Holy Spirit comes into your heart and is united with the seed of life. God created the first man from the dust and breathed into his nostrils the breath of life. The breath of life is the seed of life, the life itself. Thus, it can never die and it has been passed down to the descendants through the sperms and eggs of human beings from one generation to the next.

This seed of life is wrapped by heart. After God created

Adam, He planted the knowledge of life, the knowledge of spirit in his heart. The way a newborn baby has to learn the knowledge of this world to be a man of culture and character and live as a human being, a living being needs the knowledge of life to become a true living being even though it is already life itself.

Adam had once been filled with only the knowledge of spirit, namely the truth. However, after he disobeyed God, the communication with God was disconnected. He then began to lose the knowledge of spirit little by little, and untruth took the place in his heart.

From that time on, heart that had been filled with only truth came to be filled with two parts: truth and untruth. For example, Adam had love in his heart, but enemy the devil planted an untruth called hatred into him. As a result, as you can see in Genesis 4, Cain, to whom Adam gave birth after he committed sin, killed his brother Abel because of envy and jealousy.

As time went by, another part began to develop in the heart, which was filled with truth and untruth. That part is called "nature." You inherited the characteristics and traits from your parents. You input what you see, hear, and learn along with your feeling in your mind. These two form "nature" in the pursuit of the truth.

This nature is often called "conscience," and this is formed very differently depending on the kind of people you meet, the kind of books you read, and the kind of circumstances in which you are raised. For instance, while looking at the same event or individual, some say, "It's evil" while others may say, "It's good" or "It belongs to goodness."

Therefore, when you analyze one's heart, there are a true part that belongs to God, an untrue part that was given by Satan, and one's nature formed as the result of these two parts.

The Holy Spirit United With the Seed of Life in the Heart

In Adam's case, these three parts were wrapping the seed of life that had been given by God in heart. This state is when God's Word "You will surely die" was fulfilled after Adam ate from the tree of the knowledge of good and evil. Even though there is the seed of life, it is no different from being dead if it does not function.

For example, when you sow seeds in the field, not all the seeds sprout because some of them are already dead. Yet, if the seeds are alive, they will surely sprout.

It is the same with human beings. If the seed of life that was given by God is completely dead, it cannot revive, and there is no need for God to prepare Jesus Christ for the salvation of human beings or make heaven and hell.

However, the seed of life given to man when God breathed the breath of life into him is everlasting. When you receive the gospel, the seed of life revives; the broader the true part is in your heart, the more easily you can accept the gospel. Whoever listens to the message of the cross and accepts Jesus Christ receives the Holy Spirit. At this time, the seed of life in your heart is united with the Holy Spirit.

On the contrary, people with the conscience seared as with a hot iron have no space for the gospel to enter because the heart of untruth is completely wrapping and concealing the seed of life in their hearts. The seed of life that has been in the state of death gains power to perform its function when it combines with God's great power, the Holy Spirit.

To Become a Man of Spirit

As you attend worship services, realize God's word, and pray, God's grace and strong power come upon you and enable you to follow the nature of the Holy Spirit.

Through this process, your heart and spirit become one as your heart becomes more and more true by removing the untruth from it and filling it with the truth. If one's heart is completely filled with the knowledge of spirit and truth, this heart is spirit itself the way the first man Adam had been.

Even if you may look faithful, you act according to your nature if you do not pray. The Holy Spirit in you cannot give birth to spirit and you are still a man of flesh. Furthermore, you cannot follow the nature of the Holy Spirit if you do not break your own thoughts and arguments even though you pray very diligently or for a very long time. Therefore, you cannot be transformed into a man of spirit.

The Holy Spirit enables you to think according to the truth in your heart. That is, you live after the desires of the Holy Spirit. Accordingly, Satan works in the same way to lead you to the way of destruction by tempting you to follow the fleshly thought as much as you still have the untruth in your heart.

Therefore, you have to get rid of both fleshly thoughts and self-righteousness as it says in 2 Corinthians 10:5, *"We are destroying speculations and every lofty thing raised up against the knowledge of God, and we are taking every thought captive to the obedience of Christ."*

When you obey God's word, saying, "Yes" and follow the desire of the Holy Spirit, your heart can be filled only with truth, and then you can become a perfectly sanctified man of spirit.

You Can Receive Whatever You Ask

You become one with the Lord when you throw away all the untruth, break "self-righteousness" by giving birth to spirit with the Holy Spirit, and make your heart as clean as the heart of your Lord Jesus Christ.

A man and a woman become one flesh and give birth to a baby by the unification of a sperm and an egg. Likewise, when you come out of the world and become one with Jesus Christ, your bridegroom by accepting Him, you will give birth to spirit with the Holy Spirit and abundantly receive the blessing of being a child of God.

As it says in Romans 12:3, there are measures of faith, and you receive answers according to these measures. In 1 John 2:12 and following, the growth of faith is compared to the process of the growth of human beings.

Those who accept Jesus Christ, receive the Holy Spirit, and are saved have the faith of little children (1 John 2:12). Those who try to apply the truth into action have the faith of children

(1 John 2:13). When they grow up more from this stage and actually apply the truth into action, they have the faith of young men (1 John 2:13). If they grow up more, they have the faith of fathers (1 John 2:13).

When you read about Job from the Old Testament, God recognized him as a blameless and upright man but when Satan challenged, God allowed Satan to test Job. At first, Job insisted he was righteous. However, he soon realized his wickedness and repented before God when his evil in his nature was exposed by the test. Job's self-righteousness was broken and his heart became righteous and pure in the sight of God. Only then could God bless him twice abundantly than before.

Likewise, if you obtain the measure of fathers' faith, which is the highest stage of faith by breaking your own self-righteousness and becoming one with the Lord, you can receive overflowing blessings as a child of God. This is what God has promised you in 1 John 3:21-22: *"Beloved, if our heart does not condemn us, we have confidence before God; and whatever we ask we receive from Him, because we keep His commandments and do the things that are pleasing in His sight."*

You Can Enjoy Blessings as a Child of God

In this way, you become one with Jesus Christ to the extent that you become spiritual. You also receive the blessing of becoming one with God as much as you accomplish God's righteousness.

Jesus promised you in John 15:7 that *"If you abide in Me,*

and My words abide in you, ask whatever you wish, and it will be done for you." Also, in John 17:21, He told us *"that they may all be one; even as You, Father, are in Me and I in You, that they also may be in Us, so that the world may believe that You sent Me."*

Likewise, if you are united with the Lord by getting out of this world that is ruled by the devil's power of darkness, you become one with your Father God. On this, Galatians 4:4-7 reads as follows:

> *But when the fullness of the time came, God sent forth His Son, born of a woman, born under the Law, so that He might redeem those who were under the Law, that we might receive the adoption as sons. Because you are sons, God has sent forth the Spirit of His Son into our hearts, crying, "Abba! Father!" Therefore you are no longer a slave, but a son; and if a son, then an heir through God.*

The way people inherit possessions from their parents, you inherit the kingdom of God when you become His child by accepting Jesus Christ. That is, the children of the devil inherit Hell from the devil, and the children of God inherit heaven from God.

However, you have to keep in mind that those who do not give birth to spirit by the Holy Spirit must go to Hell because heaven is a pure place filled only with truth and that to the extent your spirit is prosperous and becomes one with God, you get the glory of residing closer to God in heaven.

Therefore, I hope you may receive the blessing of eternal life by accepting Jesus Christ your bridegroom and become one with the Lord Jesus and the Father God by throwing away all the untruth and casting away self-righteousness. In this way, you can give all the glory to God.

False Confessions Do Not Lead to Salvation

Jesus Christ becomes your true bridegroom who leads you to the way of eternal life and blessing when you are united with Him through faith. If you resemble the heart of Jesus Christ your bridegroom and attain perfect faith, you not only inherit the kingdom of heaven but you will also shine like the sun there.

When you read the Bible carefully, you find that some people who claim to believe in God are not saved. In Matthew 25, there is a parable of ten virgins. Five wise virgins who had prepared oil were saved but the other five unwise virgins could not be saved.

Likewise, God tells you clearly in the Bible who can and cannot be saved, even if every one of them may claim to have faith. You would then know the kind of life you have to live in order to be saved.

It says clearly in Matthew 7:21, *"Not everyone who says to Me, 'Lord, Lord,' will enter the kingdom of heaven, but he who does the will of My Father who is in heaven will enter."* If you call Jesus 'Lord, Lord,' it means you believe that Jesus is the Christ. However, you cannot be saved just by calling on the Lord's name and attending church on Sundays.

Evil-doers Cannot Be Saved

God tells you about the Judgment in Matthew 13:40-42:

So just as the tares are gathered up and burned with fire, so shall it be at the end of the age. The Son of Man will send forth His angels, and they will gather out of His kingdom all stumbling blocks, and those who commit lawlessness, and will throw them into the furnace of fire; in that place there will be weeping and gnashing of teeth.

When a farmer harvests, he gathers the wheat into his barn, but he burns up the chaff with fire. In the same way, God is telling you that those who are not right in God's sight must face punishment.

"All stumbling blocks" refer to all those who claim to believe in God, but tempt brothers and sisters in faith and cause them to lose their faith. Thus, you will not be saved if you cause people to sin and do evil.

What, then, is evil? 1 John 3:4 reads that, *"Everyone who practices sin also practices lawlessness; and sin is lawlessness."*

Just as every country has its own set of laws, there is a spiritual law in God's kingdom as well. The law of the spiritual realm is God's Word written in the Bible. Whoever violates God's Word is condemned the way anyone who breaks the law is prosecuted according to the law. Therefore, violating God's Word is evil and sin.

God's law can be largely divided into four categories: "do's," "don't do's," "keep's," and "cast off's." Since God is Light, He tells His children to do what is right, not to do what is wrong, keep the duties of the children of God, and cast off what God loathes because He wants His children to live in the Light.

In Deuteronomy 10:13 God urges us, *"Now, Israel, what does the LORD your God require from you, but to fear the LORD your God, to walk in all His ways and love Him, and to serve the LORD your God with all your heart and with all your soul, and to keep the LORD's commandments and His statutes which I am commanding you today for your good?"* On the one hand, you will receive blessings if you put God's Word into action. On the other hand, you will receive eternal death because of evil and sin if you do not live by His Word.

Galatians 5:19-21 remarks the works of the flesh:

Now the deeds of the flesh are evident, which are: immorality, impurity, sensuality, idolatry, sorcery, enmities, strife, jealousy, outbursts of anger, disputes, dissensions, factions, envying, drunkenness, carousing, and things like these, of which I forewarn you, just as I have forewarned you, that those who practice such things will not inherit the kingdom of God.

"Immorality" refers to all kinds of sexual impurity and not

remaining chaste, including having sexual relationship before legal marriage. "Impurity" here means disorderly actions beyond common sense resulting from the sinful nature.

"Sensuality" is when you always follow your sinful, sexual immorality and live by adulterous words and deed. "Idolatry" is worshipping objects that are made of gold, silver, bronze or any other substance, or when you love anything more than you love God.

"Sorcery" is to entice somebody with shrewd lies. "Enmities" is to have a desire to ruin other people in enmity, the opposite of love. "Strife" refers to the action of struggling to seek self-benefit and authority. "Jealousy" is to hate another person because you feel he is better than yourself. "Outbursts of anger" does not just mean being angry, but causing damage to others due to extreme anger.

"Disputes" refers to making a separate group or a branch and following the works of Satan because you do not agree with others. "Dissensions" is to make a party and separate by following your own thoughts, not the thoughts of the Holy Spirit. "Factions" refer to denying God the Trinity and Jesus who came in flesh, shed His blood to redeem human beings and became the Christ.

"Envy" is damaging or carrying out harmful actions against somebody because of jealousy. "Drunkenness" is the act of drinking alcohol, and "Carousing" means not only getting drunk, self-indulgent living, and lack of control, but also failing to perform your duties properly as a spouse or a parent.

In addition, "things like these" means there are many sinful acts similar to these, and those who perform these acts will not be saved.

Sins That Lead to Death and Sins That Do Not

In this world, "sin" is deemed a "sin" when the result of that sin is apparent and physical damage to another party is supported by sound evidence. However, God, who is Light, tells us not only sinful acts but also all the darkness that is against the light is sin.

Even though they are not displayed or witnessed, all sinful desires in your heart such as hatred, envy, jealousy, lust, judging others, condemning, heartlessness, and dishonest minds are evil and sins as well.

That is why God tells us, *"But I say to you that everyone who looks at a woman with lust for her has already committed adultery with her in his heart"* (Matthew 5:28), and *"Everyone who hates his brother is a murderer; and you know that no murderer has eternal life abiding in him"* (1 John 3:15). In addition, in Romans 14:23 it says, *"But he who doubts is condemned if he eats, because his eating is not from faith; and whatever is not from faith is sin,"* and James 4:17 reads that *"Therefore, to one who knows the right thing to do and does not do it, to him it is sin."* Therefore, you should realize that it is sin and lawlessness not to do what God wants and commands.

However, will all people die if they commit these sins? You have to realize that it is to live in faith if one who would lie before prays and tries to become a truthful man. Even if they have not yet thrown away all the dishonesty in their heart because of their weak faith, it is not true that they will not be saved because of this sin.

1 John 5:16-17 tells us, *"If anyone sees his brother committing a sin not leading to death, he shall ask and God will for him give life to those who commit sin not leading to death. There is a sin leading to death; I do not say that he should make request for this. All unrighteousness is sin, and there is a sin not leading to death."*

Sins are generally divided into two categories: the ones leading to death and the others not leading to death. Those who commit sins that do not lead to death can be saved if you encourage them, pray for them, and help them repent their sins. Yet, if one commits sins that lead to death, he cannot be saved even if you pray for him.

People considered honest sometimes lie for their own benefits, or do many deceitful deeds even if the deeds themselves do not harm other people. You come to acknowledge that you were sinners when you realize the truth, although you thought you had lived a righteous life before you believed in God. God shows you not only the sins that can be seen but also evil thoughts in your hearts, all of which are sins.

All wrongdoings are sins and the wages of sin is death. However, Jesus Christ has forgiven all your sins in the past, present, and future by shedding His blood on the cross. There are sins that can be forgiven by the power of Jesus' blood when you repent and turn away from them. These are the sins that do not lead to death.

If you do not repent but just keep on sinning, your conscience will become hardened. Then, eventually, you cannot receive the spirit of repentance if you commit a sin that leads to death. Thus, your sins cannot be forgiven even if you try to repent.

Now, let us look at the three kinds of sins that lead to death: blaspheming against the Spirit, subjecting the Son of God to open shame repeatedly, and keeping on sinning willfully.

Blaspheming the Holy Spirit

There are three things in blaspheming against the Holy Spirit. You commit blasphemy against the Spirit when you speak against the Holy Spirit, when you oppose the work of the Holy Spirit, and when you disgrace the Holy Spirit.

> *Therefore I say to you, any sin and blasphemy shall be forgiven people, but blasphemy against the Spirit shall not be forgiven. Whoever speaks a word against the Son of Man, it shall be forgiven him; but whoever speaks against the Holy Spirit, it shall not be forgiven him, either in this age or in the age to come* (Matthew 12:31-32).

> *And everyone who speaks a word against the Son of Man, it will be forgiven him; but he who blasphemes against the Holy Spirit, it will not be forgiven him* (Luke 12:10).

First, "speaking against others" is to slander them and deter their works. **"Speaking against the Holy Spirit"** is to try to hinder the accomplishment of God's kingdom by interrupting works of the Holy Spirit based on one's own will and thoughts. For example, it is speaking against the Holy Spirit when you oppose the work of God because it does not coincide with your own thoughts even though it is the work of the Holy Spirit.

If you condemn a servant of God as heretic when in fact he is not, and interrupt the works of the Holy Spirit, it is such a terrible sin before God that it cannot be forgiven. Therefore, you must be able to distinguish between spirits according to the truth.

Of course, you have to sternly warn people and must not allow their behavior if they try to make others receive evil spirit or they are truly heretic in the sight of God. Titus 3:10 reads, *"Reject a factious man after a first and second warning."*

Today, many people condemn some churches as heretic or even persecute them in many ways, which acknowledge God the Trinity and are accompanied by works of the Holy Spirit, since such people are not able to distinguish between spirits. Although they claim to believe in God, they do not have sufficient biblical knowledge on heresy. Sometimes, they do not even know the definition of heresy.

In the case of persecuting others due to the lack of proper knowledge, if people repent and turn away, they can be forgiven. However, if they disturb the works of God with an evil intent and jealousy even though they know it is the work of the Holy Spirit, they can never be forgiven.

You can find an example of this in the Bible. In Mark 3, when Jesus performed miraculous signs and wonders, those who were jealous of Him spread a rumor that He was mad. The rumor had spread so widely that His family members living in a distance came to take Him out of the public.

Scribes and the Pharisees criticized Jesus, saying, *"The scribes who came down from Jerusalem were saying, 'He is possessed by Beelzebul,' and 'He casts out the demons by the ruler of the demons'"* (Mark 3:22). They had thorough knowledge of God's Word. They knew the Law very well and taught it to people and yet they still opposed God's works due to their jealousy and envy of Jesus.

Second, "opposing the work of the Holy Spirit" is defying the voice of the Holy Spirit that God has given, or judging and condemning the works of the Holy Spirit and trying to harm other people.

For instance, it is speaking against the Holy Spirit to spread rumors or fabricate documents, or condemn a pastor or church as "heretical" where works of the Holy Spirit are shown in order to disturb revival meetings or gatherings.

Then, what does "Whoever speaks a word against the Son of Man, it shall be forgiven him" mean? "The Son of Man" in this verse refers to Jesus who came as a human being before He was crucified on the cross.

Speaking against the Son of Man means to disobey Jesus, knowing and recognizing Him merely as a person because He came in flesh. Inability to recognize Jesus as the Savior results from lack of knowledge. In this case, you will be forgiven and can be saved only if you thoroughly repent and accept the Lord.

Therefore, if you commit this kind of sin without knowing the truth or before you receive the Holy Spirit, God gives you a chance to repent and be forgiven time and again.

However, if you disobey and oppose the Lord while knowing exactly who Jesus Christ is, you must realize that you can never be forgiven for this because it is the same as speaking against the Holy Spirit and opposing the woks of the Holy Spirit.

Third, blasphemy also means disgracing things that are divine, holy, and pure. Blasphemy against the Holy Spirit also means **disgracing the Holy Spirit,** the Spirit of God, and God's divinity. It is a sin of disgracing God's eternal power and divinity if you slander the works of the Holy Spirit, saying they are works of Satan, or if you insist that something is the work of the Holy Spirit when it is not. Also, preaching the truth as untruth, claiming what is not true as if it were true, and condemning what is true as if it were fallacious are all "blasphemy against the Holy Spirit."

In the old days, if one were caught for his words or actions of blasphemy against the king, it was considered treason and he was put to death.

If you blaspheme against the holy divinity of God, who is almighty and cannot be compared with any king of this world, you can never be forgiven.

Even Jesus, who was in very nature God and came to this world in flesh, did not condemn anybody. If you still condemn brothers and sisters, and furthermore disgrace the works done by the Holy Spirit, what a terrible sin it would be! If you stand in awe and fear of God, you can never oppose, speak against, or disgrace the Holy Spirit.

Therefore, you must realize that these sins can never be forgiven either in this age or in the age to come and you should never commit these sins. Even though you have committed these sins before, you should seek God's grace and repent with all your heart.

Subjecting the Son of God to open shame

It leads you to death to crucify the Son of God all over again and subject Him to open shame, as described in Hebrews 6.

> *For in the case of those who have once been enlightened and have tasted of the heavenly gift and have been made partakers of the Holy Spirit, and have tasted the good word of God and the powers of the age to come, and then have fallen away, it is impossible to renew them again to repentance, since they again crucify to themselves the Son of God and put Him to open shame* (Hebrews 6:4-6).

Some people leave the church and God through the temptation of this world and fall into greatly disgracing God even though they have received the Holy Spirit, know that there are Heaven and Hell, and believe in the Word of truth. We say they commit a sin of crucifying the Son of God all over again and subjecting Him to public disgrace. This kind of person does not only commit many sins controlled by Satan, but also denies God and persecutes and humiliates the church and believers.

They have already handed their conscience over to Satan, so

their hearts are full of darkness.

Therefore, they would not even want to repent at all and the spirit of repentance does not come upon them. They do not have any chance to repent and therefore, they can never be forgiven.

Judas Iscariot committed this sin. He was one of Jesus' twelve disciples. He witnessed many signs and wonders, but he became greedy and sold Jesus for thirty silver coins. Later, his conscience was stricken and he was filled with regret, but the spirit of repentance did not come upon Judas. His sin could not be forgiven, and he finally committed suicide because he was greatly tormented by his guilt (Matthew 27:3-5).

Keeping on sinning willfully

The last sin that leads to death is keeping on sinning willfully after you have received the knowledge of the truth.

> *For if we go on sinning willfully after receiving the knowledge of the truth, there no longer remains a sacrifice for sins, but a terrifying expectation of judgment and the fury of a fire which will consume the adversaries* (Hebrews 10:26-27).

To "go on sinning willfully after receiving the knowledge of the truth" means repeating unlawful things that God does not forgive. Also, it means to continue sinning, knowing that it is a sin just as *"It has happened to them according to the true proverb, 'A dog returns to its own vomit,' and, 'A sow, after washing, returns to wallowing in the mire'"* (2 Peter 2:22).

On the one hand, when David, who loved God so much, committed adultery, it gave birth to many sins and led him to murder one of his most loyal soldiers. However, when Nathan the prophet pointed out his sin, King David repented immediately.

On the other hand, King Saul kept on sinning even after Samuel the prophet had pointed out his sins. David repented and received God's blessings, while Saul was forsaken because he did not repent and kept on sinning.

On the one hand, the Holy Spirit in the hearts of those who commit sins willfully fades away because God turns His back on them. They then lose their faith and do evil and wrong deeds controlled by the devil. Finally, the Holy Spirit in them will completely disappear, and they cannot be saved because they cannot repent and their names will be erased from the Book of Life (Revelation 3:5).

On the other hand, there are people who keep on committing sins because they have known God only with knowledge but do not believe in Him in their hearts. Their sins can be forgiven and they can be led to the way of salvation when they thoroughly and wholeheartedly repent and have true faith.

Therefore, you should know that you will not be saved when you commit sins willfully carrying out the works of the flesh even if you may have once been enlightened, believed that there are Heaven and Hell, and experienced God's abundant grace.

I also hope you will understand fully that all sins are lawlessness and darkness and God hates them even if some of them may not lead to death. Please be a wise believer who does not allow or commit any kind of sin.

The Flesh and the Blood of the Son of Man

In order to maintain a healthy life, you must consume appropriate food and beverages. In the same way, in order to keep your spirit healthy and gain eternal life, you must eat the flesh and drink the blood of the Son of Man.

Now, you are going to learn what the flesh and the blood of the Son of Man are, and why you must eat His flesh and drink His blood to gain eternal life, based on the following text from John 6:53-55:

> So Jesus said to them, "Truly, truly, I say to you, unless you eat the flesh of the Son of Man and drink His blood, you have no life in yourselves. He who eats My flesh and drinks My blood has eternal life, and I will raise him up on the last day. For My flesh is true food, and My blood is true drink."

What Is the Flesh of the Son of Man?

Jesus tells you in the Bible the secrets of heaven and God's will with many parables. For people living in this three dimensional world, it is very hard to understand and realize the will of God, who dwells in the four dimensional world and above. Thus, Jesus compared heavenly things to non-living things, plants, animals and lives in this world to help us better understand the divine will.

That is why Jesus the only begotten Son of God is compared to the rock and star, which are the non-dimensional, to the one-dimensional vine, to the two-dimensional lamb, and to the Son of Man who is three dimensional.

Jesus is called the Son of Man, so the flesh of the Son of Man is the flesh of Jesus.

John 1:1 tells us that, *"In the beginning was the Word, and the Word was with God, and the Word was God."* John 1:14 observes that *"And the Word became flesh, and dwelt among us, and we saw His glory, glory as of the only begotten from the Father, full of grace and truth."*

Jesus is the one who came to this world in flesh as the Word of God. Therefore, the flesh of the Son of Man is God's Word, which is the truth itself, and eating the flesh of the Son of Man is to learn God's Word in the Bible.

How to Eat the Flesh of the Son of the Man

In Exodus 12:5 and following verses, Jesus is portrayed as the "Lamb":

Your lamb shall be an unblemished male a year old; you may take it from the sheep or from the goats. You shall keep it until the fourteenth day of the same month, then the whole assembly of the congregation of Israel is to kill it at twilight. Moreover, they shall take some of the blood and put it on the two doorposts and on the lintel of the houses in which they eat it.

Generally, many believers think the lamb refers to new believers, but when you study the Bible carefully, the lamb is a symbol of Jesus.

John the Baptist, looking at Jesus who was coming towards him, said in John 1:29, *"The next day he saw Jesus coming to him and said, 'Behold, the Lamb of God who takes away the sin of the world!'"* And Peter the Apostle referred to Jesus as a lamb in 1 Peter 1:18-19, saying, *"You were not redeemed with perishable things like silver or gold from your futile way of life inherited from your forefathers, but with precious blood, as of a lamb unblemished and spotless, the blood of Christ."* Besides these, many other expressions compare Jesus to a lamb.

Why does the Bible compare Jesus to a lamb? A lamb is the mildest and the most obedient of all livestock. It recognizes the voice of its shepherd and obeys him. No one else can fool the lamb even if people try to imitate the voice of its shepherd. It gives white and soft fur, milk, meat and all parts of its body to people.

Just as a lamb sacrifices everything for mankind, Jesus obeyed God's will perfectly and sacrificed everything for us.

Jesus came to this world in flesh although He is in very nature God, preached the gospel of heaven, healed many diseases and infirmities, and was crucified. Jesus gave up everything to redeem you from your sins.

Jesus is compared to a lamb because His characteristics and

actions resemble those of a mild lamb, and eating a lamb symbolizes eating the flesh of Jesus, namely the flesh of the Son of Man.

How, then, should you eat the flesh of the Son of Man? Let us look at Exodus 12:9-10 that gives the following instruction:

> *Do not eat any of it raw or boiled at all with water, but rather roasted with fire, both its head and its legs along with its entrails. And you shall not leave any of it over until morning, but whatever is left of it until morning, you shall burn with fire.*

First, you should not eat God's Word raw

What does it mean to eat the flesh of the Son of Man "raw"?

Generally, it is not good to eat raw meat. If you eat raw meat, you may get some virus or bacteria and become sick. In the same way, God tells you not to eat God's Word raw because it is harmful.

God's Word is written by the inspiration of the Holy Spirit, so you must read it and make it your food with the inspiration of the Holy Spirit.

What if you interpret God's Word literally? You would probably misunderstand God's intention. Therefore, eating "God's Word raw" means to literally interpret the Bible.

As John 1:1 says *"The Word was God,"* the Bible contains God's heart and will and all things are accomplished according to this Word.

God's Word tells us how we can get to Heaven. You must understand God's Word fully in order to obtain eternal life. Inversely, a man of flesh cannot see or grasp the spiritual world.

It is like a cicada not knowing there is a sky when it is a grub in the ground. It is like a chicken not knowing the outer world when it is in the egg. It is like a baby not knowing anything about the world when he is still in his mother's womb.

Likewise, as long as you are in this fleshly world, you do not know anything about the spiritual world.

God is telling you that there is another world beyond this three-dimensional world. Just as an unborn chicken has to break its shell, you also have to break your own fleshly thought in order to understand and enter the spiritual realm.

For example, Matthew 6:6 reads, *"But you, when you pray, go into your inner room, close your door and pray to your Father who is in secret, and your Father who sees what is done in secret will reward you."* If you were to interpret this verse literally, you would always have to pray in your room. However, you cannot find any predecessors of faith praying in their rooms in secret.

Jesus did not pray in His room but on a mountainside spending the night (Luke 6:12), and at a solitary place early in the morning (Mark 1:35).

In addition, Daniel prayed three times a day with the windows opened towards Jerusalem (Daniel 6:10) and the apostle Peter prayed on the roof (Acts 10:9).

Then, what does it mean when Jesus said, "Go into your

inner room, close your door and pray"?

Here, a "room" spiritually symbolizes the heart of a person. So going into your inner room means passing your thoughts and going into your hearts deep inside, just as you would pass a living room or a bedroom to go into an inner room. Only then, can you pray with all your heart.

When you go into an inner room, you are isolated from the outside. Likewise, when you pray, you have to block all unnecessary thoughts, worries and concerns and pray with all your heart.

Therefore, you must not eat the flesh of the Son of Man raw. You should not interpret God's Word literally. That is, you should interpret God's Word spiritually by the inspiration of the Holy Spirit.

Second, do not eat God's Word cooked in water

What does "Do not eat any of it boiled at all with water" mean? It means that we are not to add anything to the Word of God but eat it purely.

It is not right to preach God's Word and mix it with politics, stories of the society, or adages of admired or historical individuals.

God, who created the heavens and the earth and controls mankind's life and death, blessing and curse, is almighty and does not lack anything.

1 Corinthians 1:25 says, *"Because the foolishness of God is wiser than men, and the weakness of God is stronger than men."* This is recorded to make you realize that even the wisest and the

most excellent person cannot be compared with God.

You cannot preach everything covered in the Bible in your whole life. Then, how dare you mix people's words and God's Word when you deliver message?

People's words change as time goes by. Even if there is any truth to them, they have already been said in the Bible, and they are said with God's wisdom.

Therefore, your first priority should be God's pure Word in teaching the Bible. Of course, you can give some parables or illustrations in order to make people understand God's Word and the secrets of the spiritual world more easily.

You should realize that only God's Word is everlasting and the perfect and complete truth leading you to eternal life. Thus, you should not eat His Word cooked in water.

Third, you must eat God's Word roasted with fire

What does it mean to "roast it with fire, both its head and its legs along with its entrails"? (Exodus 12:9) It means that you should make God's Word, the flesh of the Son of Man, your spiritual food wholly without leaving anything out.

For example, some people doubt the fact that Moses parted the Red Sea. Some people do not even try to read Leviticus because the sacrifices in the Old Testament are difficult to understand. Some other people say the miracles Jesus performed are hard to believe and think those miracles could only occur 2,000 years ago. They leave out many things that do not fit human thoughts and try to extract only moral lessons.

They do not even care to keep in mind such words as "Love your enemy," or "Avoid every form of evil" because those words seem too hard for them to obey. Would it be possible for them to be saved?

Therefore, you should not take only what you want from the Bible like the foolish people. You should eat all the words in the Bible wholly roasted over the fire from Genesis through Revelation.

What does it mean, then, by eating God's Word "roasted with fire"? The fire here refers to the fire of the Holy Spirit. You should be filled and inspired by the Holy Spirit when you read and listen to God's Word because it is written through the inspiration of the Holy Spirit. Otherwise, they are only knowledge, not spiritual food.

In order to eat God's Word roasted with the fire, you need to pray fervently. Prayers serve as oil to become the source of the fullness of the Holy Spirit. If you eat God's Word by the inspiration of the Holy Spirit, it is sweeter than honey. You will also never get bored even if the sermon is very long, for it is so precious and you love to listen to God's Word as a thirsty deer looking for a stream of water.

This is how to eat God's Word roasted over the fire. Only in this way will you understand God's word, make it your spiritual flesh and blood, and realize and follow God's will. This is how you give birth to spirit by the Holy Spirit, grow your faith, and recover the lost image of God by finding out the whole duty of men.

However, those who eat God's Word with their own thoughts

without roasting it over the fire feel God's Word boring, and they cannot remember it because they listen to it in idle thoughts. They can neither grow spiritually nor obtain true life.

Fourthly, you should not leave God's Word until the morning

What does it mean by "You shall not leave any of it over until morning, but whatever is left of it until morning, you shall burn with fire"?

It means that you should eat the flesh of the Son of Man, God's Word during the night. The world in which you live right now is a dark world controlled by the devil, and it can be spiritually expressed as night or nighttime. When our Lord comes again, all darkness will disappear and everything will be recovered; it will become morning, the world of light.

Therefore, "do not leave any of it over until morning" means you should learn God's Word to prepare yourself as a bride of our Lord before He returns.

In addition, whether or not the Lord's coming back is near, you live only seventy or eighty years, and you do not know when you will meet the Lord. Until you meet the Lord, you grow spiritually to the extent that you eat the flesh and drink the blood of the Son of Man. So you should diligently learn God's Word and grow spiritually.

If you have the father's faith by constantly increasing the growth of your spirit, you will receive glory like the shining sun near the throne of God in His kingdom because you know God who is from the beginning, cultivate the nine fruit of the Holy Spirit and the Beatitudes, and resemble God's image.

Drinking the Blood of the Son of Man

In order to maintain life, you must eat food along with drinking water. If you do not consume any water, the food cannot be digested and you will die. When foods go into the stomach mixed with water, they are digested, the nutrients are absorbed, and the waste is excreted.

In the same way, when you eat the flesh of the Son of Man, if you do not drink the blood of the Son of Man, you cannot digest it. Therefore, you can obtain eternal life only by eating the flesh of the Son of Man along with drinking the blood of the Son of Man.

"Drinking the blood of the Son of Man" is to put God's Word into action with faith. After you listen to the Word of God, it is very important to act accordingly, and this is faith. If you do not act according to God's Word after you have listened to it and know it, it is useless to listen to it.

The way nutrients are absorbed and the waste is excreted when you digest food, God's Word, the truth, is absorbed and the untruth is excreted when you act according to God's Word in order to purify your filthy hearts.

What are then "absorbed truth" and "excreted untruth"? Let us say you have listened to God's Word, "Do not hate, but love each other." If you make it your food and act according to it, the nutrient called love is absorbed and the waste called hatred is excreted. Your heart automatically becomes purer and more truthful by excreting dirty and filthy thoughts.

Act According to God's Word After Having Listened to It

However, if you do not act according to God's Word, you are not drinking the blood of the Son of Man. Therefore, God's Word is only a piece of knowledge in the head and you cannot be saved if you do not act according to it.

Drinking the blood of the Son of Man, acting according to God's Word, cannot be done merely by human effort. You should have the will and effort to act according to His Word, and then receive God's grace, power, and the help of the Holy Spirit by praying fervently.

If you could get rid of sin by your own efforts, Jesus need not have been crucified, and God need not have sent the Holy Spirit.

Jesus Christ was crucified to forgive your sins because you cannot solve the problem of sin by yourself, and God has sent the Holy Spirit to help you change your dirty heart to a clean heart.

The Holy Spirit, the Spirit of God, helps God's children to live within the truth and righteousness. Therefore, with the help of the Holy Spirit, the children of God should live according to God's Word getting rid of their sins and receive God's love and blessing.

Forgiveness Only by Walking in the Light

To say you are eating the flesh and drinking the blood of the Son of Man, it means you are acting in the light according to God's Word. Then, to what kind of actions does it refer? You must behave in the light. You leave the darkness and act in the light when you eat the flesh of the Son of Man, digest it, and make your heart true. When you act in the light, the blood of the Lord cleanses your sins of the past, present, and future.

Even if you have sins that are not removed yet, when you repent with your whole heart before God, your sins can be forgiven by the grace of God. Those who truly believe in God and try to accomplish the righteousness in their hearts are not sinners anymore but righteous men, and they can be saved and obtain the eternal life.

God Is Light

1 John 1:5 says that *"This is the message we have heard from Him and announce to you, that God is Light, and in Him there is no darkness at all."*

The apostle John, who wrote 1 John, was taught directly by Jesus, who had come to this world and became the Light to this world and the way to God.

Thus, it says about Jesus in John 1:4-5, *"In Him was life, and the life was the Light of men. The Light shines in the darkness, and the darkness did not comprehend it."* Jesus declared Himself, *"I am the way, and the truth, and the life; no one comes to the Father but through Me"* (John 14:6).

Therefore, the disciples of Jesus witnessed the fact that "God is Light" through Jesus, and the message they declared to you is that "God is Lght."

Light Spiritually Means Truth

What, then, is the "light"? Spiritually, light means truth and truth is the opposite of darkness.

God tells us in Ephesians 5:8, *"For you were formerly darkness, but now you are Light in the Lord; walk as children of Light."* Those who listen to the message that "God is Light" and learn the truth from God can shine and light this world, the way light drives darkness away.

The children of Light who act according to the truth bear the fruit of the Light. That is why it says in Ephesians 5:9, *"For the fruit of the Light consists in all goodness and righteousness and truth."* The spiritual love described in 1 Corinthians 13 and the fruit of the Spirit such as love, joy, peace, patience, kindness, goodness, faithfulness, gentleness, and self-control are the fruit of the Light.

Therefore, light refers to all words of truth on goodness, righteousness, and love such as "love one another, pray, keep the Sabbath, keep the Ten Commandments" that God tells you in the Bible.

Darkness Spiritually Means Sin

Darkness refers to a state in which there is no light, and it spiritually means sin.

All untrue things, which are the opposite of the truth, are such things as written in Romans 1:28-29, *"And just as they did not see fit to acknowledge God any longer, God gave them over to a depraved mind, to do those things which are not proper, being filled with all unrighteousness, wickedness, greed, evil; full of envy, murder, strife, deceit, malice."* All these are darkness.

The Bible tells you to get rid of all the things belonging to darkness such as stealing, murder, adultery and every kind of evil.

On the one hand, some people claim to be children of God, even though they do not obey what God tells them to do or keep but do the things that God tells them not to do or to throw out. This darkness is controlled by the enemy devil and Satan and it belongs to this world, so it can never be together with the light. This is why those who act in the darkness hate the light and live away from it.

On the other hand, the true children of God, who is the Light and in whom there is no darkness, should do away with the darkness and act in the Light. Only then, can you communicate with God and will everything go well in your life.

Evidence of Having a Fellowship with God

Usually, there is a very close fellowship based on love between parents and their children. In the same way, it is obvious for you—who believe in Jesus Christ—to have fellowship with God who is the Father of your spirit (1 John 1:3).

Fellowship here means not only one knowing the other, but

both of them knowing each other well. You cannot say you have a fellowship with the President even though you know a great deal about him. It is the same in your fellowship with God. In order to have a true fellowship with God, you should know Him as well as He knows and recognizes you.

1 John 1:6-7 says, *"If we say that we have fellowship with Him and yet walk in the darkness, we lie and do not practice the truth; but if we walk in the Light as He Himself is in the Light, we have fellowship with one another, and the blood of Jesus His Son cleanses us from all sin."*

This means that you have a fellowship with God only when you get rid of sins and act in the Light. If you say you have a fellowship with God while you are still acting and living in the darkness, it is a lie.

Having a fellowship with God means having a spiritual and truthful fellowship, not just having an ungodly fellowship knowing Him only with knowledge in your head. You yourself must be the light in order to have a fellowship with God because He is Light. The Holy Spirit, the heart of God, teaches you the will of God clearly to the extent that you stay in the truth so that you can have deeper communication with God when you read God's Word and pray.

If You Walk in the Darkness

You are telling a lie if you claim to have a fellowship with God but walk in the darkness committing sins. It is not walking in the truth, and you will ultimately go to the way of death.

In 1 Samuel 2, the sons of Eli the priest acted in evil and committed sins. He should have punished them, but Eli just warned them, "Why do you do such things? You should not do that."

In the end, God's anger fell upon them. Two sons of Eli the priest died in a battle, and Eli fell backward off his chair by the side of the gate; his neck was broken and he died. God's anger fell upon his descendants, too (1 Samuel 2:27-36, 4:11-22).

Therefore, as it says in Ephesians 5:11-13, *"Do not participate in the unfruitful deeds of darkness, but instead even expose them; for it is disgraceful even to speak of the things which are done by them in secret. But all things become visible when they are exposed by the light, for everything that becomes visible is light."*

If there is somebody who claims to have a fellowship with God but does not walk in the light, you should advise him with love. If he still does not come to the light, you should scold him to lead him to the light so that he will not go to the way of death.

Forgiveness by Walking in the Light

There is law in this world and when somebody violates it, he will be punished according to the measure of the act. However, he cannot help feeling guilty in his conscience because the damage has been already done even if he paid for what he has done wrong and was punished.

Likewise, you still have the sinful nature in your heart even if you accept Jesus Christ, have your sins forgiven, and are declared righteous. Therefore, God commands you to circumcise your heart so that you do not feel guilty even in your conscience.

As it says in Jeremiah 4:4, *"Circumcise yourselves to the LORD and remove the foreskins of your heart, men of Judah and inhabitants of Jerusalem, or else My wrath will go forth like fire and burn with none to quench it, because of the evil of your deeds,"* circumcision of heart means cutting off the skin of your heart.

Cutting off the skin of your heart means to follow what God says in the Bible such as, "Do's," "don't do's," "keep's," or "get rid of's." In other words, it means to drive away everything that is against God's Word such as untruth, evil, unrighteousness, lawlessness, and darkness cleaning your heart and filling them with the truth.

Therefore, you must diligently make God's Word your food, absorb the nutrients by acting according to it, and excrete the waste of evil and untruth that belong to darkness. When you circumcise your heart, you can grow up spiritually.

When you become a spiritual and truthful man excreting the sin and evil as waste, you have a fellowship with God. Then, the blood of Jesus Christ can cleanse your sins since you have this fellowship.

Therefore, you should not only accept Jesus Christ and be declared righteous, but also change into a true righteous man by eating the flesh, drinking the blood of the Son of Man, and circumcising your heart.

Faith Accompanied with
Action Is True Faith

To your surprise, you see many people who do not truly understand the meaning of faith. Some say, "Why don't you just go to church? You can still be saved."

If you listen to God's Word and know it, but do not act according to it, it is only faith as a form of knowledge in your head, not the true faith. In this manner, you cannot be saved. What is the faith that God recognizes? How can you be saved by faith?

True Repentance Requires Turning Away From Sins

1 John 1:8-9 says that *"If we say that we have no sin, we are deceiving ourselves and the truth is not in us. If we confess our sins, He is faithful and righteous to forgive us our sins and to cleanse us from all unrighteousness."*

What, then, is to confess your sins?

Let us suppose God tells you, "Going east is the way of eternal life and my will, so go east." Nevertheless, if you just keep going west and say, "God, I should go east, but I'm going west, so please forgive me," it is not a confession. This is not believing in God or fearing Him, but it is rather mocking Him. True repentance is done not only by confessing your sins with lips but also by turning away from your sins completely in your deeds. Only then does God receive it as repentance and grant you forgiveness.

The way you will die if you do not eat any food though knowing you must eat to keep your life, you are not cleansed through the blood of the Lord if you just confess your sins with your lips and do not turn away from them.

Faith without Deeds Is Dead Faith

In James 2:22, it says, *"You see that faith was working with his works, and as a result of the works, faith was perfected."* Verse 26 further goes on: *"For just as the body without the spirit is dead, so also faith without works is dead."*

Many people go to church because they have heard that there are Heaven and Hell. However, since they do not really believe in this fact in their hearts, deeds are not accompanied.

This is just faith as knowledge and dead faith.

In addition, if you confess with your lips that you believe while still living in sin, how can you say you have faith? The Bible tells you that sin committed with knowledge is worse than the sin committed without knowledge.

When you confess, "I believe" without deeds, you may think you have faith but God does not recognize this as true faith.

The Israelites who came out of Egypt experienced many works of God. God parted the Red Sea, gave them manna and quail, and protected them with the pillar of cloud by day and the pillar of fire by night.

However, when God commanded them to spy on the land of Canaan, only Joshua and Caleb believed in God's Word and power. As a result, those Israelites, who did not obey God because they did not have faith strong enough to go into Canaan, had forty years of trials in the wilderness and finally died there.

212 _ THE MESSAGE OF THE CROSS

You must realize that it is useless if you do not believe or act according to the Word of God even if you witness and experience so many works of God. Faith is completed with deeds.

Only Those Keeping the Law Are Made Righteous

God tells us in Romans 2:13 that *"For it is not the hearers of the Law who are just before God, but the doers of the Law will be justified."*

You are not righteous just by attending the service and listening to the messages. You are made righteous only when your untrue heart changes into a true heart by acting according to God's Word.

Some say you can be saved just by calling Jesus Christ "Lord" with your lips misunderstanding Romans 10:13, *"Whoever will call on the name of the Lord will be saved."* Yet, that is absolutely wrong. As it says in Isaiah 34:16, *"Seek from the book of the LORD, and read: not one of these will be missing; none will lack its mate. For His mouth has commanded, and His Spirit has gathered them,"* God's Word has the mate and it becomes perfect only when interpreted with the mate.

Romans 10:9-10 says, *"If you confess with your mouth Jesus as Lord, and believe in your heart that God raised Him from the dead, you will be saved; for with the heart a person believes, resulting in righteousness, and with the mouth he confesses, resulting in salvation."*

Only those who truly believe in their hearts that Jesus resurrected can make their confession with lips true because they live according to God's Word. They will be saved when they confess with this true faith and become increasingly righteous, but those who do not confess with this faith cannot be saved.

That is why Jesus said in Matthew 13:49-50, *"So it will be at the end of the age; the angels will come forth and take out the wicked from among the righteous, and will throw them into the furnace of fire; in that place there will be weeping and gnashing of teeth."*

Here, "the righteous" refers to all those who recognize God and claim to have faith. "Separating the wicked from among the righteous" means that those who do not act according to God's Word cannot be saved even though they attend church and lead Christian lives.

God Really Wants the Circumcision of Heart

God wants His children to be holy and perfect. That is why He tells us in 1 Peter 1:15, *"Like the Holy One who called you, be holy yourselves also in all your behavior"* and in Matthew 5:48, *"Therefore you are to be perfect, as your heavenly Father is perfect."*

During Old Testament times, people were saved by deeds as the representation of what was to come, but during New Testament times when Jesus Christ fulfilled the Law with love, you are saved by faith.

"Being saved by deeds of the Law" means that even if you have, for example, a dirty heart to murder, hate, commit adultery, lie, and so on, it is not considered sin unless it is carried out as action.

God did not condemn people unless they carried out wrong deeds because they could not cast off their sins by themselves without the Holy Spirit during Old Testament times. However, during New Testament times, you are saved only when you circumcise your heart in faith with the help of the Holy Spirit, for the Holy Spirit has come to you. The Holy Spirit makes you become aware of the difference between sin and righteousness, and the Judgment, and enables you to live according to God's Word. Therefore, you can do away with untruth and circumcise your heart with the help of the Holy Spirit.

You must realize that God really asks of you to circumcise your heart, get rid of sins, be holy, and participate in the divine nature. The apostle Paul knew this will of God and taught the circumcision of heart, not of flesh (Romans 2:28-29). He advised you to resist to the point of shedding your blood in your struggle against sin, with your eyes fixed on Jesus, the perfecter of your faith (Hebrews 12:1-4).

I hope you may have true faith accompanied by deeds realizing that you cannot enter Heaven just by calling out "Lord, Lord," but only by walking in the Light and circumcising your heart.

Chapter 9

TO BE BORN OF WATER AND THE SPIRIT

- Nicodemus Comes to Jesus
- Jesus Helps Nicodemus' Spiritual
  Understanding
- When Born of Water and the Spirit
- Three Testifiers: the Spirit, the Water,
  and the Blood

Now there was a man of the Pharisees, named Nicodemus, a ruler of the Jews; this man came to Jesus by night and said to Him, "Rabbi, we know that You have come from God as a teacher; for no one can do these signs that You do unless God is with him." Jesus answered and said to him, "Truly, truly, I say to you, unless one is born again he cannot see the kingdom of God." Nicodemus said to Him, "How can a man be born when he is old? He cannot enter a second time into his mother's womb and be born, can he?" Jesus answered, "Truly, truly, I say to you, unless one is born of water and the Spirit he cannot enter into the kingdom of God."

John 3:1-5

God sent Jesus Christ, His only begotten Son, and opened the way for salvation. Whoever accepts Him receives the right to become a child of God and enjoys a blessed and eternal life now and forever. However, nowadays you see that many people do not have this assurance of salvation even though they have received Jesus Christ. Moreover, some people claim to have received salvation but lack the faith to be saved, or some others claim to be saved because they received the Holy Spirit once, but they do not care about their deeds afterwards.

Now to conclude the message of the cross, let us be clear about how to reach the perfect salvation from the moment you receive Jesus Christ, through the story of Nicodemus.

Nicodemus Comes to Jesus

In Jesus' times, the Pharisees had a high regard for the Law of Moses, and kept holding to the tradition of the elders. They were religious leaders among the chosen Israelites who believed in God's sovereignty, the resurrection, angels, the final Judgment, and the Messiah to come.

Yet, Jesus rebuked them repeatedly, saying, "Woe to you, Pharisees." They, as hypocrites, appeared to people holy on the

218 _ THE MESSAGE OF THE CROSS

outside, but on the inside were full of greed and self-indulgence like whitewashed tombs (Matthew 23:25-36).

Nicodemus Had a Good Heart

Nicodemus was one of the Pharisees of the Jewish ruling council called Sanhedrin. However, he did not persecute Jesus unlike other Pharisees. Instead, he believed that Jesus had come from God, seeing wonders and signs Jesus performed. Nicodemus wanted to know who Jesus was because he had a good heart.

In John 7:51, Nicodemus asks the Pharisees who wanted to seize Jesus, defending Him, *"Our Law does not judge a man unless it first hears from him and knows what he is doing, does it?"*

It could not have been easy to talk in that way as a member of the Sanhedrin at that time. Even now if a government outlaws or discourages Christianity by law, official men cannot stand on the side of Christianity. Likewise, at that time the Israelites regarded all other religions except for Judaism as false. Nicodemus knew that he might be excommunicated if he stood on the side of Jesus.

Nevertheless, Nicodemus defended Jesus. It proved that he was truthful and that he stood firm in faith in Jesus.

John 19:39-40 portrays a scene immediately after the death of Jesus on the cross:

Nicodemus, who had first come to Him by night, also

came, bringing a mixture of myrrh and aloes, about a hundred pounds weight So they took the body of Jesus and bound it in linen wrappings with the spices, as is the burial custom of the Jews.

Therefore, Nicodemus believed that Jesus was a man of God, served Jesus unchangingly even after His crucifixion, and gained salvation with faith in His resurrection.

Nicodemus Comes To Jesus

In John 3, there is a dialogue between Jesus and Nicodemus before he understood the truth in spirit.

One night Nicodemus came to Jesus, and professed, *"This man came to Jesus by night and said to Him, 'Rabbi, we know that You have come from God as a teacher; for no one can do these signs that You do unless God is with him'"* (v. 2).

Nicodemus at first did not know that Jesus was the Messiah and Son of God. However, after he witnessed Jesus' miracles, Nicodemus realized and professed Jesus was a man of God because he had a good conscience. Through his good conscience, he knew that it was only the Almighty God who could raise the dead, let the blind see, let the cripple stand, and let the leper be healed.

Then, why did he come to Jesus at night? He was like those people who do not want to attend church openly because they do not have confidence in God the Creator.

Although Nicodemus had a good heart, he did not have true

faith. He did not have confidence in Jesus as the Son of God and Messiah, so he did not visit Jesus in the daytime openly - he did so at nighttime.

Jesus Helps Nicodemus' Spiritual Understanding

Jesus told Nicodemus, *"Jesus answered and said to him, 'Truly, truly, I say to you, unless one is born again he cannot see the kingdom of God'"* (John 3:3).

However, Nicodemus could not understand this at all. Then he asked again, "How can a man be born when he is old?" He did not have a spiritual faith, so he wondered, "An old man dies and returns to soil, and then how can he be born again?"

Then Jesus told him about being born of water and the Spirit: *"Truly, truly, I say to you, unless one is born of water and the Spirit he cannot enter into the kingdom of God. That which is born of the flesh is flesh, and that which is born of the Spirit is spirit"* (vv. 5-6).

When Nicodemus was curious about what Jesus said, Jesus explained it in a parable: *"The wind blows where it wishes and you hear the sound of it, but do not know where it comes from and where it is going; so is everyone who is born of the Spirit"* (v. 8).

After Adam's disobedience, every man's spirit died and everyone thereafter was destined to die. However, a man's spirit revives after being born of the Holy Spirit. As he becomes spiritual, he restores the image of God and is saved. Yet, Nicodemus did not understand what Jesus meant (v. 9).

So he asked, "How can this be?" Jesus responded:

> *If I told you earthly things and you do not believe, how will you believe if I tell you heavenly things? No one has ascended into heaven, but He who descended from heaven: the Son of Man. As Moses lifted up the serpent in the wilderness, even so must the Son of Man be lifted up; so that whoever believes will in Him have eternal life* (vv. 12-15).

In Numbers 21:4-9, the Israelites who had been led out of Egypt spoke against Moses because their journey to Canaan was becoming increasingly difficult to bear. Then God turned His face away and sent venomous snakes that bit people.

As they cried out for help, God told Moses to make a bronze snake and put it up on a pole. God saved whoever looked at it, but stubborn people died because they did not even bother to look at it in disbelief.

To Understand the Word of God Spiritually

Why did God command to make a bronze snake and put it up on a pole? From Genesis 3:14 we know the snake was cursed. In addition, Galatians 3:13 says, *"Cursed is everyone who hangs on a tree."*

Therefore, putting a bronze snake up on a pole symbolizes

that Jesus would be put on a wooden cross like a cursed snake to redeem you. In addition, just as whoever looked at the bronze snake lived, whoever believes in Jesus Christ is saved.

Nicodemus could not understand the meaning of the Word of God, because he was not yet born of water and the Spirit, and his spiritual eyes were not yet opened.

Even today, unless you are born of water and the Spirit and spiritual eyes are opened, you cannot understand the meaning of a spiritual message because you may take it literally and misunderstand it.

You have to pray fervently in order to understand the spiritual meaning of the Word of God by the inspiration of the Holy Spirit. Then the God of grace will open your heart, and you can understand the Word of God and have true faith.

When Born of Water and the Spirit

Jesus told Nicodemus when he visited at night, *"Truly, truly, I say to you, unless one is born of water and the Spirit he cannot enter into the kingdom of God. That which is born of the flesh is flesh, and that which is born of the Spirit is spirit"* (John 3:5-6).

Let us be clear about the meaning of being born of water and the Spirit. How can you be born again by water and the Spirit and obtain salvation?

Water Symbolizes the Water of Eternal Life

Water relieves your thirst and smoothes the inner organs of the body. It also cleanses your body both outside and inside.

Thus Jesus compared the water of eternal life to water to explain that it cleanses you and brings life.

Jesus tells us in John 4:14, *"But whoever drinks of the water that I will give him shall never thirst; but the water that I will give him will become in him a well of water springing up to eternal life."*

If you drink water, you are not thirsty for a while, but you eventually become thirsty again. Water in this scripture means eternal water. Whoever drinks the water that Jesus gives will never be thirsty again. Namely, "a well of water springing up to eternal life" gives you life.

John 6:54-55 reads, *"He who eats My flesh and drinks My blood has eternal life, and I will raise him up on the last day. For My flesh is true food, and My blood is true drink."* That is, Jesus' flesh and His blood are eternal water.

Moreover, His "flesh" refers to the Word of the Bible because Jesus is the Word who came to the world in flesh. The eating of His flesh refers to keeping His Word in your mind through reading the Bible.

The blood of Jesus is life, and the life is the truth. The truth is Christ, and Christ is the power of God. All these are the blood of Jesus. Since the power of God comes in faith, drinking the blood of Jesus means to obey His Word by faith.

You learned that water spiritually symbolizes Jesus' flesh—

that is the Word of God and Lamb of God. The way water cleanses your body, the Word of God washes dirty things away from your heart.

That is why you are baptized by water in the church, and baptism symbolizes that you are a child of God and forgiven of your sins. Furthermore, it means that you should meditate on the Word of God and be cleansed by it everyday.

Born Again With Water

How, then, can you wash off dirt from your heart by the Word of God that is eternal water?

There are four types of commands God gives us: "Do's," "Don't do's," "Keep something," and "Cast off something." For example, God told you not to do such things like envy, hatred, judging, stealing, adultery, and murder.

In the same manner, you should not do what is forbidden and at the same time, you should cast off every kind of evil things. You should also keep the Sabbath, evangelize, pray, and love one another. Your heart will then gradually be filled with the truth by the help of the Holy Spirit, and the Word of God will wash away your unrighteousness or sin. In this way, your heart can be circumcised and transformed into the truth by acting in accordance with the Word of God, and this is "being born of water."

Therefore, in order to receive whole salvation, you should not only accept Jesus but also circumcise your heart by obeying God's Word every moment of your life.

Born Again With the Spirit

To receive salvation, you should be born of water and of the Spirit as well. How can you be born of the Spirit? In Acts 19:2, the apostle Paul asked some disciples, *"Did you receive the Holy Spirit when you believed?"* What is to receive the Holy Spirit?

The first man Adam consisted of "spirit," "soul," and "body" (1 Thessalonians 5:23), but his spirit died as a result of disobedience. Then he became a being that is no better than an animal made of soul and body (Ecclesiastes 3:18).

If you repent your sins, acknowledging that you are a sinner, God gives you the Holy Spirit as a gift and as a token that you are His child (Acts 2: 38).

Any children of God, who receive the Holy Spirit, are able to distinguish between good and evil by the Word of God and to live according to the Word of God by the power and strength from heaven through their fervent and continuous prayer.

In this way, you change into the truth and have spiritual faith to the extent that you give birth to spirit through the Holy Spirit. In John 3:6 it says, *"That which is born of the flesh is flesh, and that which is born of the Spirit is spirit,"* and John 6:63 observes, *"It is the Spirit who gives life; the flesh profits nothing; the words that I have spoken to you are spirit and are life."*

Become a Man of Spirit Following the Holy Spirit

When you are born of water and the Holy Spirit, you come

to obtain a citizenship in heaven (Philippians 3:20). As God's child, you attend worship services, praise Him with joy, and strive to live in the light.

Prior to receiving the Holy Spirit, you lived in the darkness because you did not know the truth. However, after you receive the Holy Spirit, you try to live in the light.

As time goes on, you find that while you have joy in your heart, you are constantly struggling within. It is because the law of the Spirit that follows the desires of the Holy Spirit struggles against the law of sinful nature that has followed the lust of the flesh, the lust of the eyes, and the boastful pride of life (1 John 2:16).

The apostle Paul talked about this struggle: *"For I joyfully concur with the law of God in the inner man, but I see a different law in the members of my body, waging war against the law of my mind and making me a prisoner of the law of sin which is in my members. Wretched man that I am! Who will set me free from the body of this death?"* (Romans 7:22-24)

When you are born of water and the Spirit, you have just become a child of God. It does not mean that you are a spiritually perfect person.

That is why Galatians 5:16-17 tells us, *"But I say, walk by the Spirit, and you will not carry out the desire of the flesh. For the flesh sets its desire against the Spirit, and the Spirit against the flesh; for these are in opposition to one another, so that you may not do the things that you please."*

In order to follow the Holy Spirit, you should live according to the Word of God and do the will acceptable and pleasing to

God. Thus, if you follow the desires of the Spirit, you will not be tempted and will be able to defeat the enemy devil and Satan who tempt you to follow the desires of the sinful nature. You can live by the truth and devote yourself faithfully to God's kingdom and His righteousness.

When you follow the desires of the Holy Spirit, you are in joy and peace. However, you will be wretched and burdened when you follow the desires of sinful nature.

As your faith matures, you can cast off your sins and follow the desires of the Holy Spirit in all matters. The desires in you that want to follow the sinful nature will disappear. Moreover, you do not need to struggle to cast off sins and to be wretched anymore. You can be always joyful under any circumstances.

God is pleased with those who live by the desires of the Spirit. He gives them the desires of their hearts as He promises us in Psalm 37:4, *"Delight yourself in the LORD; and He will give you the desires of your heart."*

If you change your heart into one filled only with truth, God is very pleased with you and makes everything possible for you. I hope that you will be born of water and the Spirit, and live in accordance with the desires of the Spirit.

Three Testifiers: the Spirit, the Water, and the Blood

As I explained already, you should be born of water and the Spirit to be saved. However, to receive complete salvation, you must be purified from sins with the blood of Jesus by walking in the light.

If your heart is not purified, you still have sins. Therefore, you need the blood of Jesus Christ to be purified from the remaining sin.

On this, 1 John 5:5-8 tells us the following:

> *Who is the one who overcomes the world, but he who believes that Jesus is the Son of God? This is the One who came by water and blood, Jesus Christ; not with the water only, but with the water and with the blood. It is the Spirit who testifies, because the Spirit is the truth. For there are three that testify: the Spirit and the water and the blood; and the three are in agreement.*

Jesus Comes by Water and Blood

John 1:1 reads that *"The Word was God"* and John 1:14, *"And the Word became flesh, and dwelt among us, and we saw His glory, glory as of the only begotten from the Father, full of grace and truth."* That is, Jesus, God's only Son and the very Word of God, came to earth in flesh to forgive our sins. Even today, He continues to purify us with the Word of God - the Bible.

However, you cannot live according to the Word of God without the help of the Holy Spirit. It is impossible to cast off sins by your own strength. You should receive the help of the Holy Spirit through the fervent prayer so that you can remove the lust of the flesh, the lust of the eyes, and the pride of life. Only then can you drive away the darkness of untruth from your heart.

In addition, you need the shedding of blood to be forgiven. In Hebrews 9:22 it says that *"And according to the Law, one may almost say all things are cleansed with blood, and without shedding of blood there is no forgiveness."* You need Jesus' blood because only His blameless and spotless blood gives you forgiveness.

You must believe in Jesus who came in water and blood, and receive the Holy Spirit as a gift from God to obtain salvation, for which you need the following three: the Spirit, the water and the blood.

If there is no shedding of the blood, there is no forgiveness and you are still in sin. You need not only the Word—the water—to be purified, but also the Holy Spirit to help you live according to this Word completely. So these three are in agreement.

Therefore, we should, after being forgiven of our sins by accepting Jesus Christ, continue to be born of water and the Spirit in order to gain perfect salvation, understanding the fact that three of the Spirit, the water and the blood altogether saves us and leads us to Heaven.

Chapter 10

WHAT IS HERESY?

- The Biblical Definition of Heresy
- The Spirit of Truth and the Spirit
  of Error

"But false prophets also arose among the people, just as there will also be false teachers among you, who will secretly introduce destructive heresies, even denying the Master who bought them, bringing swift destruction upon themselves. Many will follow their sensuality, and because of them the way of the truth will be maligned; and in their greed they will exploit you with false words; their judgment from long ago is not idle, and their destruction is not asleep."

2 Peter 2:1-3

'As the civilization of materialism has developed, people came to deny God because they depend on their wisdom and knowledge. As sins have spread, people's spirits became darkened and people became corrupt. Therefore, many people are deceived by lies because they cannot distinguish between what is true and what is false. They also make the mistake of judging other people based on their own righteous knowledge and theories.

In Matthew 12:22-32, Jesus healed a demon-possessed man who had been blind and mute. However, when the Pharisees heard of this, they said, *"This man casts out demons only by Beelzebul the ruler of the demons"* (v. 24). They deemed God's work to have been carried out by a demon.

Jesus said to them in Matthew 12:31-32, *"Therefore I say to you, any sin and blasphemy shall be forgiven people, but blasphemy against the Spirit shall not be forgiven. Whoever speaks a word against the Son of Man, it shall be forgiven him; but whoever speaks against the Holy Spirit, it shall not be forgiven him, either in this age or in the age to come."*

The Pharisees concluded that what Jesus had done by the power of God was the work of a demon. This is blasphemy opposing the Holy Spirit. These Pharisees, therefore, could not possibly be forgiven.

If you distinguish between truth and falsehood clearly by the Bible, you will not judge other people nor be deceived by what is false.

Let us delve further into "heresy" from God's perspective, how to distinguish between God's Spirit and evil ones, and some heretical sects with which you need to be cautious.

The Biblical Definition of Heresy

The Oxford Dictionary defines 'heresy' as 'a belief or an opinion that is against the principles of a particular religion.'

Paul, Charged as a Ringleader of a Heretical Sect

Acts 24:5 reads that *"For we have found this man a real pest and a fellow who stirs up dissension among all the Jews throughout the world, and a ringleader of the sect of the Nazarenes."* Here "the sect of the Nazarenes" refers to "a heretical sect," and this is the first time that the word "heretic" appears in the Bible.

The Jews brought charged against Paul before the governor because they thought that the gospel Paul was preaching was heretical. Paul refuted the accusation and professed his faith as recorded in Acts 24:13-16.

> *Nor can they prove to you the charges of which they now accuse me. But this I admit to you, that according*

to the Way which they call a sect I do serve the God of our fathers, believing everything that is in accordance with the Law and that is written in the Prophets; having a hope in God, which these men cherish themselves, that there shall certainly be a resurrection of both the righteous and the wicked. In view of this, I also do my best to maintain always a blameless conscience both before God and before men.

Was Paul the Apostle Really a Heretic?

You should look up the definition of heresy in the Bible because the Bible is the Word of God, the only true Being who can distinguish truth from falsehood. The definition of heresy is discussed in 2 Peter 2:1:

But false prophets also arose among the people, just as there will also be false teachers among you, who will secretly introduce destructive heresies, even denying the Master who bought them, bringing swift destruction upon themselves.

"The Master who bought them" refers to Jesus Christ. Man originally belonged to God and lived according to His will. After his disobedience, however, Adam became a sinner belonging to the devil. However, God had pity on people who were on the path to death. God sent Jesus, His only Son, as a peace offering and allowed Him to be crucified so that He could open the way of salvation through His blood.

God worked for us, who had once belonged to the devil, to have our sins forgiven if we believe in Jesus Christ. We also receive life and come to belong to God again. This is why we can say that Jesus bought us by His crucifixion, and the Bible tells you that Jesus is "the Master who bought them."

Heretics Deny Jesus Christ

Now you know the "heretic" refers to "those who deny the Master who bought them, bringing swift destruction upon themselves" (2 Peter 2:1). This term had never been used until Jesus completed His mission as the Savior. The name "Jesus" means "[the one who] will save His people from their sins." "Christ" is "The Anointed One." Jesus became the Savior only after He had done His work – to be crucified and raised.

That is why you cannot find this term in the Old Testament or in the Gospels of Matthew, Mark, Luke, and John in which Jesus' life is recorded. Even the Pharisees, scribes, and priests who persecuted Jesus did not use that term. Neither was it used by the chief priests.

Only after Jesus resurrected to accomplish His mission as the Christ, "people denying the Master who bought them" appeared. And only then, did the Bible start cautioning us about these heretics.

Therefore, if people believe in Jesus Christ as "the Master who bought them," they are not heretics. If they deny that, however, they are heretics.

The apostle Paul did not deny Jesus Christ who had purchased him with His precious blood. Instead, Paul gave thanks to Jesus Christ whom he proclaimed wherever he went, and Paul was persecuted and had to pay a high price. Five times, he received from the Jews the forty lashes minus one. Once he was stoned. He was imprisoned, persecuted by Gentiles and his own countrymen, and was betrayed by those whom he had trusted. Despite all this, Paul became a man of great power by overcoming those sufferings with joy and gratitude, and glorified God by healing countless people in the name of Jesus Christ until the day he died a martyr's death.

Paul Preached the Gospel Demonstrating God's Power

You should know that God's power cannot be shown by those who deny God the Creator and Jesus Christ who is in very nature God because the Bible explicitly says, *"Once God has spoken; twice I have heard this: that power belongs to God"* (Psalm 62:11).

You must not judge a person who demonstrates God's power because that power proves that God is with him and that the person loves Him greatly. In Galatians 1:6-8, Paul, who was called a ringleader of the Nazarene sect, strictly cautions not to follow or preach a different gospel other than the message of the cross:

I am amazed that you are so quickly deserting Him

*who called you by the grace of Christ, for a different
gospel; which is really not another; only there are some
who are disturbing you and want to distort the gospel of
Christ. But even if we, or an angel from heaven, should
preach to you a gospel contrary to what we have
preached to you, he is to be accursed!*

Even today, some people are deemed heretics, even though
they never deny Jesus Christ but only preach the gospel of Christ
and proclaim the living God by demonstrating and working with
His power.

Do Not Randomly Judge Others as Heretical

I have also suffered and endured a series of trials by being
accused of heresy, as I demonstrated God's power and my church
grew bigger. In fact, the size of congregation has grown to more
than 120,000 members in the past thirty-four years since the
church was founded in 1982.

I had suffered from many diseases for seven years, and was
healed by the power of God at one time. Then I tried to live for
the glory of God whether I ate or drank the way Paul the apostle
did. I put my life in God's hand and focused it on "Only Jesus,
always Jesus."

From the time I was a layman, I tried to testify that God had
healed me and to preach the gospel. After being called as a
servant of God, I preached the message of the cross and
proclaimed the living God and Jesus the Savior. I even testified

about God when I officiated at a wedding because I eagerly wanted to lead more people to the way of salvation.

I realized that both the powerful Word of God and the evidence of the living God were necessary to be the witness of the Lord to the ends of the world. So I prayed ardently, as the ancestors of faith did, to receive the power of God, and passed all trials given to me with gratitude and joy.

Sometimes there were deathlike trials. However, as Jesus received the glory of resurrection after His blameless death, God increased my power in accordance with His will whenever I overcame trials one by one.

As a result, every time I testified why God is the only true God and why you are saved when you believe in Jesus Christ all over the world—in Kenya, Uganda, Honduras, Japan, even the heavily Muslim Pakistan and the Hinduism-dominant country India—since 2000, tens of thousands of people repented, the blind received sight, the mute spoke, the deaf heard, and incurable diseases such as AIDS and various cancers were healed. These miracles greatly glorified God.

Therefore, one who fully understands what heresy is does not judge others as heretics carelessly. In Acts 5:33-42, you read about Gamaliel, a teacher of the Law, who was honored by all the people. How did he act?

At that time, the Pharisees of the Sanhedrin forbade Peter and John to testify about Jesus Christ, but they were full of the Holy Spirit and did not obey the council. Thus, the Sanhedrin members wanted to put the apostles to death. Yet, Gamaliel stood up in the Sanhedrin and ordered that the men be put outside for a while. Then He addressed them:

> *Men of Israel, take care what you propose to do with*
> *these men. For some time ago Theudas rose up,*
> *claiming to be somebody, and a group of about four*
> *hundred men joined up with him. But he was killed, and*
> *all who followed him were dispersed and came to*
> *nothing. After this man, Judas of Galilee rose up in the*
> *days of the census and drew away some people after*
> *him; he too perished, and all those who followed him*
> *were scattered. So in the present case, I say to you, stay*
> *away from these men and let them alone, for if this plan*
> *or action is of men, it will be overthrown; but if it is of*
> *God, you will not be able to overthrow them; or else you*
> *may even be found fighting against God* (Acts 5:35-39).

As you read this passage, you realize that if a miraculous work were not from or of God, it would fail at last even if people take no action to stop it. Yet, even if they oppose or disturb the works that are from God, they will not be able to stop those works. Instead, their effort is no different from fighting against God and they will be subject to His punishment and judgment.

Sometimes people judge others as heretics because of differences in interpretation of the Bible, visions from the Holy Spirit, and even tongues although they all acknowledge the Trinity and that Jesus Christ came in flesh.

Some people even say that they do not need the tongues or visions, and these Holy Spirit's works are wrong because there is no record that Jesus spoke in tongues or saw visions. However, the Bible says these are good for us:

> *But to each one is given the manifestation of the Spirit for the common good. For to one is given the word of wisdom through the Spirit, and to another the word of knowledge according to the same Spirit; to another faith by the same Spirit, and to another gifts of healing by the one Spirit, and to another the effecting of miracles, and to another prophecy, and to another the distinguishing of spirits, to another various kinds of tongues, and to another the interpretation of tongues. But one and the same Spirit works all these things, distributing to each one individually just as He wills* (1 Corinthians 12:7-11).

Consequently, you should not slander or judge those who have different kinds of gift of the Spirit as heretics just because you do not experience them yourself.

The Spirit of Truth and the Spirit of Error

In 2 Peter 2:1-3, there is an explanation about heresy. The Bible cautions you about false prophets and teachers who secretly introduce destructive heresies. *"Many will follow their sensuality, and because of them the way of the truth will be maligned; and in their greed they will exploit you with false words; their judgment from long ago is not idle, and their destruction is not asleep"* (2 Peter 2:2-3).

Also in 1 John 4:1-3, it says, *"Beloved, do not believe every spirit, but test the spirits to see whether they are from God, because many false prophets have gone out into the world. By this you know the Spirit of God: every spirit that confesses that Jesus Christ has come in the flesh is from God; and every spirit that does not confess Jesus is not from God; this is the spirit of the antichrist, of which you have heard that it is coming, and now it is already in the world."*

Test Each Spirit Whether or Not It Is From God

There are good spirits belonging to God that lead you to salvation while there are also evil spirits that deceive you to destruction.

On the one hand, one who is given the Spirit of God acknowledges that Jesus Christ came in flesh. He believes in the Trinity—God, Jesus Christ, and the Spirit, so he is sealed as a child of God. He can understand the truth and live according to the truth with the help of the Spirit.

On the other hand, one who has the spirit of the antichrist opposes Jesus Christ with the Word of God and denies His redemption. You have to be careful and be able to distinguish antichrists because an antichrist often works among believers by misusing God's Word.

In any case, denying Jesus Christ is no different from fighting against God who sent Him to this world.

The Bible warns about the antichrist in 2 John 1:7-8 as follows:

For many deceivers have gone out into the world, those who do not acknowledge Jesus Christ as coming in the flesh. This is the deceiver and the antichrist. Watch yourselves, that you do not lose what we have accomplished, but that you may receive a full reward.

In 1 John 2:19 is another warning for us:

They went out from us, but they were not really of us; for if they had been of us, they would have remained with us; but they went out, so that it would be shown that they all are not of us.

There are two types of antichrist: the man who is possessed by the spirit of antichrist and the man who is deceived by the spirit of the antichrist. They both try to deceive men wherever the Holy Spirit dwells. They capture men to oppose the Word of God and deceive them through their thoughts. People whose thoughts are thoroughly controlled by the spirit of the antichrist are called "demon-possessed."

If a minister were given the spirit of the antichrist, church members keep advancing towards the way to destruction captured by the spirit of the antichrist.

Therefore, you have to know clearly about the Spirit of truth and the spirit of error in order not to be deceived by the spirit of the antichrist but to live according to the truth and the light.

How to Distinguish the Spirits

1 John 4:5-6 reads, *"They are from the world; therefore they speak as from the world, and the world listens to them. We are from God; he who knows God listens to us; he who is not from God does not listen to us. By this we know the spirit of truth and the spirit of error."*

The term "error" refers to "a false statement that is untrue." The spirit of error is the worldly spirit that deceives you into believing what is untrue as though it were true, and it makes you leave the boundaries of faith. Namely, one who is from God listens to the Word of truth, but one who belongs to the world listens to worldly sayings, not the truth. Thus, it is easy to recognize them. It becomes obvious to you whether it is the light or the darkness if you know the truth. Then you can say, "This person is in the truth but that person is in the darkness."

For example, if one says on Sunday, "Let's go on a picnic in the afternoon. Let's attend the morning service only. Isn't that just as good?" or if he tries to destroy God's kingdom making evil tricks and still claims to believe in God, that is the work of the spirit of error.

You may understand many things that God freely gives you if you receive the Spirit of truth who is from God (1 Corinthians 2:12). That is why the Holy Spirit dwells in you—God's precious child. He is the Spirit of truth and guides you into all truth. He does not speak on His own; He speaks only what He hears, and He will tell you what is yet to come.

Therefore, Jesus says in John 14:17, *"That is the Spirit of truth, whom the world cannot receive, because it does not see Him or know Him, but you know Him because He abides with you and will be in you."* John 15:26 gives us another reminder of the Holy Spirit: *"When the Helper comes, whom I will send to you from the Father, that is the Spirit of truth who proceeds from the Father, He will testify about Me."*

Also 1 Corinthians 2:10 reads, *"For to us God revealed them through the Spirit; for the Spirit searches all things, even the depths of God."* As it is written, the Holy Spirit is the only one who wholly knows and perceives God's mind.

Consequently, those who received the Spirit of truth listen to the Word of truth and obey it. The more God's kingdom and His righteousness are extended, the more they rejoice. They are full of life, longing for the heavenly kingdom.

Yet, some simply attend church without joy because they do not possess God-generated faith. They still belong to the world and prefer worldly things such as money and amusement. Thus, they cannot live in the truth, long for the heavenly kingdom, or love God wholeheartedly.

Ultimately, these people leave God by the spirit of error because they belong to the world and do not have the Spirit of truth. Also, if somebody slanders or gossips about other brothers and sisters of faith or disturbs others in envy from being faithful to God's kingdom and His righteousness, he is not from the Spirit of truth.

Let No One Lead You Astray

1 John 3:7 urges us as follows: *"Little children, make sure no one deceives you; the one who practices righteousness is righteous, just as He is righteous."* You should not turn away from God's Word so that you will not be deceived by untruthful knowledge because nothing but the Word of God can teach you. Only then, will you receive the complete salvation, be prosperous in this world, and enjoy the eternal life in the heavenly kingdom.

However, the devil makes every effort to prevent God's children from living by the Word, and makes you compromise with the world, turn away from God, doubt Him, and oppose Him. In 1 Peter 5:8 it says, *"Be of sober spirit, be on the alert. Your adversary, the devil, prowls around like a roaring lion, seeking someone to devour."*

How then can the enemy devil and Satan deceive children of God? You can assimilate this to a woman who is tempted by a man. If a woman carries herself with grace and dignity, and behaves in a well-mannered way, men cannot dare tempt her. Otherwise, man can easily tempt her who does not behave appropriately. Likewise, the enemy devil and Satan will approach the one who does not stand firm in the truth and is doubtful of God. The devil tempts these people to turn away from God and oppose Him and in the end leads them into the way of death. Eve was also tempted by the devil because she was caught off-guard by twisting God's Word.

Of course, you may encounter trials even though you have no

fault. This is because God wants to bless you, the way you can see in Daniel's trial of being thrown into the lions' den or Abraham's trial of sacrificing his son as a burnt offering.

When you face trials or difficulties because you do not firmly stand on the truth, you should immediately turn from your sins with repentance, drive out all temptations and trials with the Word of God, and try your best to stand firmly on the rock of truth.

Stand Firm in the Truth; Do Not Be Deceived

In 1 Timothy 4:1-2, the author writes, *"But the Spirit explicitly says that in later times some will fall away from the faith, paying attention to deceitful spirits and doctrines of demons, by means of the hypocrisy of liars seared in their own conscience as with a branding iron."*

This refers to later times during which some people who claim to have faith will turn away from their faith by following deceiving spirits and things taught by demons.

The deceived are hypocritical even if their doings seem faithful and righteous. They pray before others, and try to be faithful because of money, not in gratitude of God's grace. At last, they abandon their faith and go to the way of death because their consciences are seared as with a hot iron by lying, living without the truth, and indulging worldly amusement.

God strictly cautions you through the Bible not to be deceived. Jesus warns us in Matthew 7:15-16: *"Beware of the false prophets, who come to you in sheep's clothing, but inwardly are ravenous wolves. You will know them by their fruits. Grapes are not gathered from thorn bushes nor figs from thistles, are they?"*

One's words and action reflect his thoughts and will. That is, you are able to recognize people by their fruit. If someone has the fruit of evil such as hatred, envy and jealousy instead of the fruit of the truth, goodness, and righteousness, he is a false prophet.

Many false prophets, the antichrist, are already present in this world. Therefore, the children of God need to have a sound understanding on heresy, and distinguish between the spirit of truth and the spirit of error.

The enemy devil and Satan never miss the opportunity to deceive God's children and make them sin whenever they falter from the truth. When you are stable in the truth and obey it, you will not be deceived by the spirit of error, but will defeat it easily even if it approaches you.

You must not admit or adhere to any other teachings or be deceived by those teachings, which are against the truth. Instead, obey the Word of God and follow the desires of the Holy Spirit so that you may be courageous and blameless at the Second Coming of our Lord Jesus Christ.

Jesus tells us that *"The good man brings out of his good treasure what is good; and the evil man brings out of his evil treasure what is evil. But I tell you that every careless word that people speak, they shall give an accounting for it in the day of judgment. For by your words you will be justified, and by your words you will be condemned"* (Matthew 12:35-37).

The good man has a good heart and cannot cause evil and harm to other people, regardless of whether or not the act is advantageous for himself.

However, the evil man cannot rejoice in the truth. He brings every kind of evil to stumble others out of his envy and jealousy. Even though his sayings seem to be right and just, you cannot say he is a good man if he intends to speak ill of others or alienate a person from another.

Therefore, you always have to pray and be watchful so that you will not be deceived. You must be able to distinguish whether sprits are true or not and never judge others. Moreover, you should stand in faith in the Trinity—the Father, the Son, and the Spirit, believe the whole Bible, and obey and live by it.

"Come, Lord, Jesus!"

The Author
Dr. Jaerock Lee

Dr. Jaerock Lee was born in Muan, Jeonnam Province, Republic of Korea, in 1943. While in his twenties, Dr. Lee suffered from a variety of incurable diseases for seven years and awaited death with no hope for recovery. However one day in the spring of 1974 he was led to a church by his sister and when he knelt down to pray, the living God immediately healed him of all his diseases.

From the moment he met the living God through that wonderful experience, Dr. Lee has loved God with all his heart and sincerity, and in 1978 he was called to be a servant of God. He prayed fervently with countless fasting prayers so that he could clearly understand the will of God, wholly accomplish it and obey the Word of God. In 1982, he founded Manmin Central Church in Seoul, Korea, and countless works of God, including miraculous healings, signs and wonders, have been taking place at his church ever since.

In 1986, Dr. Lee was ordained as a pastor at the Annual Assembly of Jesus' Sungkyul Church of Korea, and four years later in 1990, his sermons began to be broadcast in Australia, Russia, and the Philippines. Within a short time many more countries were being reached through the Far East Broadcasting Company, the Asia Broadcast Station, and the Washington Christian Radio System.

Three years later, in 1993, Manmin Central Church was selected as one of the "World's Top 50 Churches" by the *Christian World* magazine (US) and he received an Honorary Doctorate of Divinity from Christian Faith College, Florida, USA, and in 1996 he received his Ph. D. in Ministry from Kingsway Theological Seminary, Iowa, USA.

Since 1993, Dr. Lee has been spearheading world evangelization through many overseas crusades in Tanzania, Argentina, L.A., Baltimore City, Hawaii, and New York City of the USA, Uganda, Japan, Pakistan, Kenya, the Philippines, Honduras, India, Russia, Germany, Peru, Democratic Republic of the Congo, Israel and Estonia.

In 2002 he was acknowledged as a "worldwide revivalist" for his powerful ministries in various overseas crusades by major Christian newspapers in Korea. In particular was his 'New York Crusade 2006' held in Madison Square Garden, the most famous arena in the world. The event was broadcast to 220 nations, and in his 'Israel United Crusade 2009', held at the International Convention Center (ICC) in Jerusalem he boldly proclaimed Jesus Christ is the Messiah and Savior.

His sermons are broadcast to 176 nations via satellites including GCN TV and he was listed as one of the 'Top 10 Most Influential Christian Leaders' of 2009 and 2010 by the popular Russian Christian magazine *In Victory* and news agency *Christian Telegraph* for his powerful TV broadcasting ministry and overseas church-pastoring ministry.

As of May of 2016, Manmin Central Church has a congregation of more than 120,000 members. There are 10,000 branch churches world-wide including 56 domestic branch churches, and more than 102 missionaries have been commissioned to 23 countries, including the United States, Russia, Germany, Canada, Japan, China, France, India, Kenya, and many more so far.

As of the date of this publishing, Dr. Lee has written 104 books, including bestsellers *Tasting Eternal Life before Death, My Life My Faith I & II, The Message of the Cross, The Measure of Faith, Heaven I & II, Hell, Awaken, Israel!*, and *The Power of God*. His works have been translated into more than 76 languages.

His Christian columns appear on *The Hankook Ilbo, The JoongAng Daily, The Chosun Ilbo, The Dong-A Ilbo, The Hankyoreh Shinmun, The Seoul Shinmun, The Kyunghyang Shinmun, The Korea Economic Daily, The Korea Herald, The Shisa News,* and *The Christian Press.*

Dr. Lee is currently leader of many missionary organizations and associations. Positions include: Chairman, The United Holiness Church of Jesus Christ; Permanent President, The World Christianity Revival Mission Association; Founder & Board Chairman, Global Christian Network (GCN); Founder & Board Chairman, World Christian Doctors Network (WCDN); and Founder & Board Chairman, Manmin International Seminary (MIS).

Heaven I & II

A detailed sketch of the gorgeous living environment the heavenly citizens enjoy and beautiful description of different levels of heavenly kingdoms.

Tasting Eternal Life Before Death

A testimonial memoirs of Dr. Jaerock Lee, who was born again and saved from the valley of the shadow of death and has been leading a perfect exemplary Christian life.

Hell

An earnest message to all mankind from God, who wishes not even one soul to fall into the depths of hell! You will discover the never-before-revealed account of the cruel reality of the Lower Grave and Hell.

My Life My Faith I & II

Dr. Jaerock Lee's autobiography provides the most fragrant spiritual aroma for the readers, through his life extracted from the love of God blossomed in midst of the dark waves, cold yoke and the deepest despair.

The Measure of Faith

What kind of a dwelling place, crown and reward are prepared for you in heaven? This book provides with wisdom and guidance for you to measure your faith and cultivate the best and most mature faith.

Spirit, Soul, and Body I & II

A guidebook that gives the reader spiritual understanding of spirit, soul, and body, and helps him find what kind of 'self' he has made so that he can gain the power to defeat darkness and become a person of spirit.

Awaken, Israel

Why has God kept His eyes on Israel from the beginning of the world to this day? What kind of His providence has been prepared for Israel in the last days, who await the Messiah?

Seven Churches

The letter to the seven churches of the Lord in the book of Revelation is for all the churches that have existed up until now. It is like a signpost for them and a summary of all the words of God in both Old and New Testaments.

Footsteps of the Lord I & II

An unraveled account of secrets about the beginning of time, the origin of Jesus, and God's providence and love for allowing His only begotten Son Passion and resurrection!

The Power of God

A must-read that serves as an essential guide by which one can possess true faith and experience the wondrous power of God

Lightning Source UK Ltd.
Milton Keynes UK
UKHW010731170621
385673UK00001B/123